DAYS OUT
WITH KIDS

SOUTH EAST
EDITION

GW00402261

DAYS OUT

WITH KIDS

TRIED-AND-TESTED FUN FAMILY OUTINGS IN THE SOUTH EAST

JANET BONTHRON

BON•BON
PUBLISHING

First published in 2000 by

Bon•Bon Publishing
24 Endlesham Road
London SW12 8JU

Copyright © Bon•Bon Publishing 2000

Cover Photographs:
Front cover © Bon•Bon Publishing 2000
Back cover shows Fishers Farm Park © Bon•Bon Publishing, and Odds Farm Park ©
Odds Farm Park

The right of Janet Bonthron to be identified
as the author of this work has been asserted by her in
accordance with the Copyright, Designs and Patents Act 1988.

A catalogue record for this book is available from the
British Library.

Every effort has been made to ensure the accuracy of
information in this book. Details such as opening times
and prices are subject to change and the authors and
publishers cannot accept liability for any errors or
omissions.

ISBN   1-901411-30-3

Design by Caroline Grimshaw
Illustrations by Sam Toft

Printed & bound in Finland by
WS Bookwell, Juva

Contents

Introduction   **5**
How To Use This Book   **7**
Map   **10**
Planning Guide   **12**

Animal Encounters

Bocketts Farm Park   **15**
Bowmans Open Farm   **18**
Burpham Court Farm Park   **21**
Drusillas Zoo Park   **24**
Fishers Farm Park   **27**
Godstone Farm   **30**
Horton Park Children's Farm   **33**
Odds Farm Park   **36**
Wimpole Home Farm   **39**
Woodside Farm & Wild Fowl Park   **42**

Look! Look! Look!

Barleylands Farm Museum	45
Bekonscot Model Village	48
Bentley Wildfowl & Motor Museum	51
Birdworld	54
Brighton Sea Life Centre	57
Cotswold Wildlife Park	60
Didcot Railway Centre	63
Roald Dahl's Children's Gallery	66
Syon Park Butterfly House & Aquatic Centre	69
Woburn Safari Park	72

The Great Outdoors

Audley End House & Country Park	75
Blenheim Palace	78
Groombridge Place Gardens	81
Hatfield House	84
Knebworth House	87
Painshill Park	90
Penshurst Place	93
Wisley RHS Gardens	96

Somewhat Historical

Amberley Industrial Museum   **99**
Bodiam Castle   **102**
Chatham World Naval Base   **105**
The Chiltern Open Air Museum   **108**
Cutty Sark & Maritime Museum   **111**
Hever Castle   **114**
Mountfichet Castle & Toy Museum   **117**
Museum of Kent Life   **120**
Weald & Downland Open Air Museum   **123**

Up, Down, There & Back

The Bluebell Railway   **126**
Colne Valley Railway   **129**
Hollycombe Steam Collection & Gardens   **132**
Kent & East Sussex Steam Railway   **135**
Leighton Buzzard Railway   **138**
The Watercress Line   **141**

The Sun Has Got His Hat On

Ham House   **144**
Kew Gardens   **147**
Littlehampton Beach   **150**
Polesden Lacey   **153**
Scotney Castle Gardens   **156**
Whitstable   **159**
Windsor Town & Great Park   **162**

Introduction

WELCOME TO DAYS OUT WITH KIDS, WRITTEN FOR PEOPLE WITH children in the South East. Now in its seventh edition, it is packed with ideas for fun family outings. With lots of outings to try and updated information for 2000/2001, I hope that it will help you tackle some of those perennial problems:

WHAT ARE WE GOING TO DO TODAY?
As a mother of four children, I know how important it is to get out of the house some days. Equally, how difficult it can be to think of places to go for a change; places that are not too far; where everyone can have a good time; where young children will be well catered for. This book gives you a personal selection of great outings to choose from; if you go out on one or two a month, there are well over a year's worth of different trips inside!

BUT WHERE IS REALLY GOOD?
Often these days it is not a problem knowing about places to go, but rather whether those places will really be a good trip for people with children. If you've no time to sift through leaflets, or don't know anyone who's been themselves then it can be daunting to try something new. The outings featured in Days Out With Kids have all been done personally, by mothers with children in tow. They are all tried-and-tested recommended trips: we've been there ourselves!

WHAT ABOUT MUMS AND DADS TOO?
If the prospect of yet another adventure playground bores you, then you'll welcome something different. Our aim has been to describe outings enjoyed by everyone in the family, with something to appeal to adults as well as children. So, some of the trips may look like just adult outings, but they're not. We want to introduce you to some of the unusual and fun places we have been to as a family. You may all get something different out of the day, but that doesn't matter, as long as you all have a good time.

HOW ARE PLACES SELECTED FOR THE BOOK?

We have included a variety of trips: for the winter and the summer, for rain and sunshine, some nearby, some a greater distance. Some of the trips are old favourites, many times visited. Others were suggested by friends as places that they love. We have noted what childcare facilities are provided in each case: pushchair accessibility, high chairs, nappy tables etc., but haven't selected places purely on this basis. Rather, the facilities information is given on the principle that if you know in advance what is provided you can plan your day accordingly.

All trips were done anonymously. No one has paid to be included in the book, and the views and opinions expressed are very much personal thoughts and reactions. Places are in the book because we had a good time there, and think that other people with children could too.

WHAT AGES OF CHILDREN ARE COVERED?

The book is aimed at people with babies, toddlers and school-aged children. Many of the trips will also appeal to children up to early teens, and, of course, adults too!

The facts given for each outing have been checked rigorously. However, things do change, and please check details (particularly opening times) before you set out.

SPECIAL EVENTS?

Finally, we have been working on our web site. Check it out on **www.daysoutwithkids.co.uk** for extra information on special events and 'hot tips' selected for the current season or month.

JANET BONTHRON
BON•BON VENTURES
24 ENDLESHAM ROAD
LONDON SW12 8JU

How To Use This Book

EACH SECTION OF THE BOOK COVERS TRIPS WHICH FALL INTO THE same broad category of attraction. Outings are described alphabetically within the section. If you know what sort of outing you want to do, then just look at the section titles, read the section summaries below, and flick through the entries included in that section. Alternatively, the handy planning guide is a rapid, self-explanatory table for identifying the right trip for you.

ANIMAL ENCOUNTERS covers farms and other birds and beasties type places which give a chance for you to have close contact with the animals. Children and animals are a winning combination, and there are plenty of places around the South East which offer it. We have chosen those which we think are distinctive in some way; for example, superb handling opportunities for children, wonderful setting, or imaginatively-displayed animals. Try them all for variety!

LOOK! LOOK! LOOK! features places with exhibitions or displays which children should particularly enjoy, including those with a travelling theme, wild or unusual creatures, tractors and even a miniature world. These outings all offer the chance for children to see something unusual or to experience at close quarters something they may only have seen on television.

THE GREAT OUTDOORS is about trips which are all or mostly outdoors in character, in an especially beautiful or quiet setting. Ideal for walks and strolls, with plenty to see for adults whilst the kids run around exhausting themselves. Couldn't be better!

SOMEWHAT HISTORICAL attractions all have a bygone age theme. Your children may not fully appreciate the historical connotations, but will be able to enjoy the setting and exhibits, whilst you can wallow in romantic nostalgia!

UP, DOWN, THERE AND BACK has outings which involve rides, both on steam trains and fairgrounds. Puffs of steam and the smell of smoke in the air are always thrilling and the ones we have included have features which make them particularly accessible. Eat your heart out, Thomas the Tank Engine!

THE SUN HAS GOT HIS HAT ON includes picnic spots that are obviously just a small selection of what is available. Most good picnic spots tend to be closely guarded secrets, but these are ones which are favourites of ours. There is something about spreading your blanket on the ground and unpacking boxes and plates of picnic food that is just pure summertime, and you can't beat it. Happy munching! Of course, many of the locations in the previous sections are also excellent picnic spots.

IF YOU DON'T MIND WHAT SORT OF ATTRACTION YOU GO TO, BUT HAVE other criteria (such as the weather, distance, or means of transport, for example) which you need to satisfy, then the best way to use the book is to refer to the map and planning guide given on the following pages. These should help you to pick a suitable day out.

THE PLANNING GUIDE can help you select an outing by distance, prevailing weather, admittance to dogs, accessibility by public transport or opening hours. ***Free,** or particularly **good value,** trips are asterisked (those costing £15.00 or less for a family of four).

Distances are approximate, and taken from Central London. We have erred on the generous side when deciding on the **wet weather** suitability – if there is somewhere to duck inside during an occasional shower then we say 'yes' under the wet weather trip heading. 'No' means, in our view, it would really be quite a miserable trip if it is raining. For people with **dogs**, 'yes' may mean on a lead only, so always take a lead.

With **public transport** accessibility we have indicated whether it is available, but you may need to do a short walk too in some cases. 'None' means that it would really be hard work going there without a car.

The planning guide also indicates whether **opening** periods are restricted (i.e. if a place is not open all the year, and/or only on some days of the week). For attractions cited as 'all year' opening, this excludes Christmas Day, Boxing Day and New Year's Day, so check first if you want to go on these days.

Once you have identified a trip that sounds appealing, refer to the detailed description for further information. Page numbers are given in the Planning Guide. The Fact File which accompanies each entry gives the address and telephone number, travel directions and distances, opening times and prices, and an indication of specific facilities (high chairs, nappy change areas and eating places). Where appropriate, the Fact File also suggests other nearby attractions.

Map

ANIMAL ENCOUNTERS | PAGE
1 Bocketts Farm Park — 15
2 Bowmans Open Farm — 18
3 Burpham Court Farm Park — 21
4 Drusillas Zoo Park — 24
5 Fishers Farm Park — 27
6 Godstone Farm — 30
7 Horton Park Children's Farm — 33
8 Odds Farm Park — 36
9 Wimpole Home Farm — 39
10 Woodside Farm & Wild Fowl Park — 42

LOOK! LOOK! LOOK!
11 Barleylands Farm Museum — 45
12 Bekonscot Model Village — 48
13 Bentley Wildfowl & Motor Museum — 51
14 Birdworld — 54
15 Brighton Sea Life Centre — 57
16 Cotswold Wildlife Park — 60
17 Didcot Railway Centre — 63
18 Roald Dahl's Gallery — 66
19 Syon Park Butterfly House & Aquatic Centre — 69
20 Woburn Safari Park — 72

THE GREAT OUTDOORS
21 Audley End House & Country Park — 75
22 Blenheim Palace — 78
23 Groombridge Place Gardens — 81
24 Hatfield House — 84
25 Knebworth House — 87
26 Painshill Park — 90
27 Penshurst Place — 93
28 Wisley RHS Gardens — 96

SOMEWHAT HISTORICAL | PAGE
29 Amberley Industrial Museum — 99
30 Bodiam Castle — 102
31 Chatham World Naval Base — 105
32 The Chiltern Open Air Museum — 108
33 Cutty Sark & Maritime Museum — 111
34 Hever Castle — 114
35 Mountfichet Castle & Toy Museum — 117
36 Museum of Kent Life — 120
37 Weald & Downland Open Air Museum — 123

UP, DOWN, THERE & BACK
38 The Bluebell Railway — 126
39 Colne Valley Railway — 129
40 Hollycombe Steam Collection & Gardens — 132
41 Kent & East Sussex Steam Railway — 135
42 Leighton Buzzard Railway — 138
43 The Watercress Line — 141

THE SUN HAS GOT HIS HAT ON
44 Ham House — 144
45 Kew Gardens — 147
46 Littlehampton Beach — 150
47 Polesden Lacey — 153
48 Scotney Castle Gardens — 156
49 Whitstable — 159
50 Windsor Town & Great Park — 162

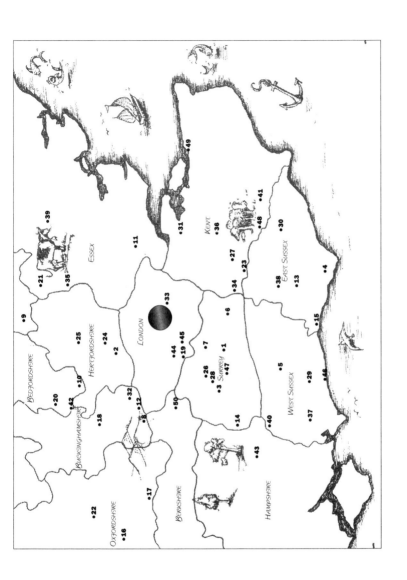

Planning Guide

OUTING	DISTANCE (MILES)	WET WEATHER TRIP	DOGS	PUBLIC TRANSPORT	OPEN	PAGE
ANIMAL ENCOUNTERS						
BOCKETTS FARM PARK*	20	YES	NO	YES	ALL YEAR	15
BOWMANS OPEN FARM*	30	NO	NO	YES	ALL YEAR	18
BURPHAM COURT FARM PARK*	30	NO	NO	YES	ALL YEAR	21
DRUSILLAS ZOO PARK	54	YES	NO	YES	ALL YEAR	24
FISHERS FARM PARK	50	NO	NO	NO	ALL YEAR	27
GODSTONE FARM*	20	NO	NO	YES	ALL YEAR	30
HORTON PARK CHILDREN'S FARM*	20	YES	NO	YES	ALL YEAR	33
ODDS FARM PARK*	25	YES	NO	YES	RESTRICTED	36
WIMPOLE HOME FARM & HALL*	55	YES	NO	NONE	RESTRICTED	39
WOODSIDE FARM & WILD FOWL PARK*	35	NO	NO	YES	RESTRICTED	42
LOOK! LOOK! LOOK!						
BARLEYLANDS FARM MUSEUM*	35	YES	YES	NONE	RESTRICTED	45
BEKONSCOT MODEL VILLAGE*	30	NO	NO	YES	RESTRICTED	48
BENTLEY WILDFOWL & MOTOR MUSEUM	50	NO	NO	NONE	RESTRICTED	51
BIRDWORLD	40	NO	NO	YES	ALL YEAR	54
BRIGHTON SEA LIFE CENTRE	50	YES	NO	YES	ALL YEAR	57
COTSWOLD WILDLIFE PARK	60	NO	YES	NONE	ALL YEAR	60
DIDCOT RAILWAY CENTRE	53	YES	YES	YES	RESTRICTED	63
ROALD DAHL'S GALLERY*	40	YES	NO	YES	RESTRICTED	66
SYON PARK BUTTERFLY HOUSE & AQUATIC CENTRE	12	YES	NO	YES	ALL YEAR	69
WOBURN SAFARI PARK	45	YES	NO	NONE	RESTRICTED	72
THE GREAT OUTDOORS						
AUDLEY END HOUSE & COUNTRY PARK*	55	NO	NO	NONE	RESTRICTED	75
BLENHEIM PALACE*	70	NO	YES	NONE	RESTRICTED	78
GROOMBRIDGE PLACE GARDENS	40	NO	NO	YES	RESTRICTED	81
HATFIELD HOUSE	20	NO	NO	YES	RESTRICTED	84
KNEBWORTH HOUSE	35	NO	YES	YES	RESTRICTED	87
PAINSHILL PARK*	25	NO	NO	YES	RESTRICTED	90
PENSHURST PLACE*	45	NO	NO	YES	RESTRICTED	93
WISLEY RHS GARDENS	20	NO	NO	YES	RESTRICTED	96

OUTING	DISTANCE (MILES)	WET WEATHER TRIP	DOGS	PUBLIC TRANSPORT	OPEN	PAGE
SOMEWHAT HISTORICAL						
AMBERLEY INDUSTRIAL MUSEUM	55	YES	YES	YES	RESTRICTED	99
BODIAM CASTLE*	55	YES	NO	NONE	RESTRICTED	102
CHATHAM WORLD NAVAL BASE	40	YES	YES	YES	RESTRICTED	105
THE CHILTERN OPEN AIR MUSEUM*	25	YES	YES	YES	RESTRICTED	108
CUTTY SARK & MARITIME MUSEUM*	15	YES	NO	YES	ALL YEAR	111
HEVER CASTLE	30	YES	YES	YES	RESTRICTED	114
MOUNTFICHET CASTLE & TOY MUSEUM	35	NO	NO	YES	RESTRICTED	117
MUSEUM OF KENT LIFE*	40	YES	YES	YES	RESTRICTED	120
WEALD & DOWNLAND OPEN AIR MUSEUM	50	YES	YES	YES	RESTRICTED	123
UP, DOWN, THERE & BACK						
THE BLUEBELL RAILWAY	45	YES	YES	YES	RESTRICTED	126
THE COLNE VALLEY RAILWAY*	60	YES	NO	NONE	ALL YEAR	129
HOLLYCOMBE STEAM COLLECTION & GARDENS	45	YES	NO	YES	RESTRICTED	132
KENT & EAST SUSSEX STEAM RAILWAY	70	YES	YES	YES	RESTRICTED	135
LEIGHTON BUZZARD RAILWAY*	40	YES	YES	NONE	RESTRICTED	138
THE WATERCRESS LINE	45	YES	YES	YES	RESTRICTED	141
THE SUN HAS GOT HIS HAT ON						
HAM HOUSE*	15	NO	NO	YES	RESTRICTED	144
KEW GARDENS	10	NO	NO	YES	ALL YEAR	147
LITTLEHAMPTON BEACH*	60	NO	YES	YES	ALL YEAR	150
POLESDEN LACEY*	30	NO	YES	NONE	ALL YEAR	153
SCOTNEY CASTLE GARDENS*	45	NO	NO	NONE	RESTRICTED	156
WHITSTABLE*	55	NO	YES	YES	ALL YEAR	159
WINDSOR TOWN & GREAT PARK*	25	YES	YES	YES	ALL YEAR	162

Animal Encounters

Bocketts Farm Park

IF YOU THINK YOU'VE HAD ENOUGH OF SQUELCHING AROUND MUDDY fields, trailing after elusive chickens or rabbits, think again. Bocketts is really very good, being extremely well-equipped to deal with families. It has plenty of animals, a host of related activities, a great tearoom and you can even have a good time there in the rain as many of the attractions are under cover.

One of the best features of the farm is that the animals are very accessible to children. They are mostly kept in small enclosures in a very large open barn, and within the barn there is a melange of different creatures – greedy goats, sleepy calves, squealing piglets, sheep and donkies. As it is a

> **"As it is a working farm, different animals are inside the barn depending on the time of year"**

working farm, different animals are inside the barn depending on the time of year. A big barn at the back is full of ewes in spring waiting to lamb, so there's a good chance of seeing them being born, or at least having a go at bottle-feeding. Separate areas house smaller animals such as rabbits, guinea pigs, ducklings and chicks who can be cuddled at touch times.

Bags of feed are on sale at the entrance for 35p a bag, so children will always have a chance to get involved. Farm staff are around to talk to, and there are loads of information plaques everywhere. There is plenty of space for pushchairs between the different enclosures.

Outside the barns there is also a lot to see and do.

Tame and beautiful red deer live in a small area next to the barn and you can follow a short walk on a broad path (suitable for pushchairs) around the fields to see horned cows, billy goats and more pigs.

The playground is great, with an enormous sandpit and a special digging area with sit-on mechanical diggers. There are old tractors to climb on, hay bales and a two-storey Wendy house as well as the usual swings, slide and wooden adventure area. At weekends, and during holidays and the summer there are tractor trailer and pony rides (small extra charge).

If they tire of the playground or it is raining, the hay bale mountain back in the barn is a fantastic alternative, with bales to scramble all over and under. Even crawling babies can enjoy playing with the hay. Next to the hay bales is a mini-tractor race track for toddlers

When you've had enough retire to the spacious and attractive 18th century barn which serves homemade lunches and teas. There is a children's menu, lots of high chairs, and a small play area with toys. On sunny days nobody seems to mind if some of the toys migrate outside to the large yard. If you want to picnic there are both covered and open areas outside with tables and benches. In one corner of the yard there is a large sandpit, so there's a chance you might be able to relax a moment with your cuppa.

If you fancy a bit of peace and quiet at the end of your visit, follow the newly-opened woodland walk on a quiet circular walk round the farm boundaries. It starts from the lower car park and is 4km long, although it can be shortened (we walked for about an hour). We were too noisy for the deer, foxes and badgers who apparently inhabit the woods but we did see some fine views and spectacular fungi!

All through the year you'll find lots of different activities going on at Bocketts, especially during the school holidays and half terms. One final point – get here early at these peak times, as it is popular, so can get busy. And justly so!

Fact File

● ADDRESS: Bocketts Farm Park, Young Street, Fetcham, near Leatherhead, Surrey
● TELEPHONE: 01372 363764
● WEBSITE: www.bockettsfarm.co.uk
● DIRECTIONS: Take A3 and A24. Signposted from the Leatherhead roundabout on the A24
● PUBLIC TRANSPORT: Train to Leatherhead or Fetcham from Waterloo, and short taxi ride
● DISTANCE: 20 miles
● TRAVEL TIME: 50 minutes
● OPENING: Daily 10.00am-6.00pm
● PRICES: Adults £3.65, children (3-17 years) £3.20, children (2 years) £2.30, under-2's free
● RESTAURANT FACILITIES: Yes
● NAPPY CHANGING FACILITIES: Yes
● HIGH CHAIRS: Yes
● DOGS: No
● PUSHCHAIR-FRIENDLY: Yes
● NEARBY: Box Hill, a few miles along the A24, has some good picnic spots with great views

Bowmans Open Farm

With an Oink, Oink here,
and an Oink, Oink there

BOWMANS IS A WORKING DAIRY AND PIG FARM WITH NO PRETENSIONS of hiding the daily routine of real farm life. It is easy to get to, has special animal demonstrations and offers the chance to see how farm life really is.

However, as you go in, your first sight will be of the distinctly 'unrural' Adventure play area. This is large, with a bouncy castle, pulley rides, tractors to climb on and a separate play area for the under-8's. It has picnic tables, a view overlooking the lake, and is ideal for picnics: it even has barbecues provided (bring your own charcoal and you can buy meat at the farm shop). If you can persuade your children to wait, leave it until the end, because the more representative aspects of farm life are further on round the Farm Trail.

"The weaned piglets crowded together like teenagers in a disco"

Plan to see the milking demonstration which takes place in the afternoon in the milking shed (see the notice at entrance for times). You can watch from a viewing platform as the cows are milked in batches of 10 at a time. It is a very streamlined operation, with the cows coming in, being fed and washed, and then the automatic milking machines attached. Watch the milk flowing through the pipes as you muse on the interesting snippets of information on the display boards. (How many tonnes of effluent the herd produces during the winter?) With no time for anyone to play up, perhaps you'll pick up a few tips for the morning 'getting to school' routine! Don't forget to give Ben the Shire horse a stroke in the stable next to the milking shed while you are there.

Make for the falconry demonstrations too. These go

on between 1.00pm and 3.00pm weekends and holidays, and give a wonderful close-up view of the birds skimming along the ground, gliding in flight and catching food mid-air. We saw hawks, owls and falcons when we were there.

Apart from the set-time displays, there is lots more to see and do. There are piglets throughout the year, both indoors in the piggery, and out in the fields. Walk over the bridge to inspect the weaned piglets in their weaning parks: crowded together like teenagers in a disco, they gave us a noisy and enthusiastic welcome.

Somewhat quieter was the calving shed, where there were several newborn calves to admire. With some heavily pregnant cows waiting alongside though, the action can hot up on occasions. Although cows usually don't calve during visiting time, it is not unknown, so be prepared!

☞   For contact opportunities check out the Touch Barn at set times of the day where you'll be able to cuddle many of the animals that young children love: lambs, kid goats, calves, rabbits, guinea pigs, chicks and even piglets. There is also a Pets' Corner outside, but here you will have more difficulty stroking the animals as, in the case of rabbits at least, they can hop away.

To see more of the commercial pig herd and all the arable side of the farm, hop on behind a tractor and go for a ride round the farm for 50p per person (under-3's free). The ride takes 20 minutes and is good fun. Children under 12 are not allowed on without an adult. Finally, if there is time and you want to see more there is a lakeside walk you can follow. It takes about half an hour and you'll see lots of fishermen and waterfowl.

With working tractors in action, farm machinery stacked about, and outbuildings dotted all over the place there is little chance to escape the reality of farm life. Go for it, but remember your wellies!

Fact File

- ADDRESS: Bowmans Farm, Coursers Road, London Colney, St Albans, Hertfordshire
- TELEPHONE: 01727 822106
- DIRECTIONS: Junction 22 of M25, towards St Albans. Signposted from roundabout next to the motorway
- PUBLIC TRANSPORT: Tube to High Barnet (Northern Line), and 84 bus to London Colney. Alight at the Bull Pub and 5-minute walk
- DISTANCE: 30 miles
- TRAVEL TIME: 1 hour
- OPENING: Daily 10.00am-5.30pm
- PRICES: Adults £4.00, children £3.00, under-3's free
- RESTAURANT FACILITIES: Yes
- NAPPY CHANGING FACILITIES: Yes, in Ladies Toilet
- HIGH CHAIRS: Yes, no straps
- DOGS: No
- PUSHCHAIR-FRIENDLY: Yes
- NEARBY: RAF Mosquito Aircraft museum (01462 483307)

Burpham Court Farm Park

Do YOUR CHILDREN EVER WISH THEY HAD COUSINS WHO LIVE ON A farm? The sort of place where they're welcome to join in and where the natural rhythm of the day always requires another pair of small hands? Burpham Court Farm could be the answer to their dreams, an unassuming family farm, whose owners have deliberately maintained a low key appeal, and where you are always welcome to join in with the feeding and putting the animals away for the night.

You enter through a traditional farmyard area surrounded by old tile-hung barns – although the yard itself is full of trikes and toy tractors as well as a real old tractor. All the traditional farm animals are here, many of them rare breeds. In the spring there are plenty of young animals to "ooh" and "aah" over, lambs to be bottle-fed every four hours, goat kids, ducklings and chicks. On a quiet day you may even see a lamb being born. Buy bags of food at the entrance (30p) for feeding the chickens and sheep.

> **"Don't miss putting the ducks to bed. It caused much hilarity amongst our lot"**

The farm trail takes about 30 or 40 minutes to walk round and gives you a chance to see all the animals in the outlying paddocks. There is a nice balance of wild and tame: it starts with a 20-minute nature walk along the banks of the Wey. Although too difficult with a pushchair, there are proper stiles to clamber over, high overgrown plants all around and plenty of treasures to take home or save for the school nature table: feathers, seed pods, leaves and sticks. Look out for hops, burdock with its spiky sticky seeds, and exploding Touch Me Not (extraordinary seed capsules that ping away from you when you flick the stem). Next to the river is a haven for wildlife too: woodpeckers, ducks, dragonflies and butterflies, especially in the height of summer.

Away from the river, the trail moves into open paddocks with wide grassy paths. Rare breeds of sheep, cattle and goats are to be found here – too numerous to mention. Our favourites were the 'teddy bear sheep' (actually Southdowns) with their incredibly thick wool, a sheep shearer's nightmare I imagine. Meanwhile, cows with long corkscrew horns peered at us dimly over the fences, sending the children running in thrilled terror.

Look for the trap door in the fairy rings and then race on down to the duck pond. Shallow and muddy, it is a

toddlers' delight (remember those wellies). Don't miss putting the ducks to bed. It caused much hilarity amongst our lot: the farmer striding out resolutely with an unruly crew of excited children and noisy ducks in his wake. Apart from the thrill for children of feeling they are really joining in on the farm, it gives you a chance to go into the barns with the ducks and collect any eggs left there. Between 4.00pm and 6.00pm most of the animals are brought in from the paddocks for the night, so you can accompany the farmer as he does his rounds and help put all the animals to bed if you want. In April and May you may get involved with sheep-shearing, and in July there is hay-making.

Back at the farm yard, go next door into the farmhouse for tea, or picnic in the yard. Real, fresh farm eggs can be bought at the shop, you may even have collected them yourselves!

Fact File

● ADDRESS: Burpham Court Farm Park, Clay Lane, Jacob's Well, Guildford, Surrey
● TELEPHONE: 01483 576089
● DIRECTIONS: A3 towards Guildford, taking the Burpham and Merrow exit before you get to Guildford. Straight over the first roundabout, right at the second, straight over the third. The farm is then on the left
● PUBLIC TRANSPORT: No. 34 bus from Guildford to Jacob's Well village hall. 10-minute walk
● DISTANCE: 30 miles
● TRAVEL TIME: 40 minutes
● OPENING: Daily 10.00am-6.00pm
● PRICES: Adult £3.25, children £2.25, under-2's free
● RESTAURANT FACILITIES: Yes
● NAPPY CHANGING FACILITIES: No
● HIGH CHAIRS: Yes
● DOGS: No
● PUSHCHAIR-FRIENDLY: Yes
● NEARBY: Clandon Park at West Clandon (01483 222482) an 18th century house and garden

Drusillas Zoo Park

THE ANIMALS HERE HAVE ALL BEEN SELECTED FOR THEIR APPEAL TO young children and the zoo lives-up well to its own description as 'the best small zoo in the country', both in terms of the child-sized animals there and the compact, manageable area to walk around. But it really distinguishes itself by having simply masses of animal activities. It was very popular when we went, during the summer holidays, and pretty hectic, so it might be best to try and avoid busy times.

The zoo is imaginatively laid-out with a succession of different themed areas: evolution, farm animals, climbing animals, Australian outback, Beaver country, Parrot Pools, and Grey Owl's cabin. You can walk through a bat house where the bats may actually fly around your head, although they were hanging upside-down asleep when we visited. New in 2000 is the Millenium Bug exhibition, full of interesting and endangered creepy crawlies. All the animals may be viewed easily and there are cut-outs in the sides of some enclosures so those in pushchairs can see too. You can even crawl into one of the enclosures through a

"Oodles of special events through the school holidays"

tunnel and pop up inside a large dome for real eyeball-to-eyeball contact with a troop of Meerkats. All the displays are great fun and really bring the zoo to life.

Participation and understanding of the animals are encouraged with lots of brain-teasers, quizzes and physical tests. Children are invited to try hanging like a monkey on poles, milking a very life-like cow or running as fast as a llama on all-fours. The Sprint Test, which gives you an immediate output of your running speed, was popular with adults too.

Feeding periods, animal encounters (owls, rats, snakes or spiders, if you dare!), and the baby animals are all good reliable entertainment for kids, so check the

DOWN ON THE FARM!

times at the entrance. The Keepers' Talks are an extra 50p per person. There are oodles of special events through the school holidays too, including animal antics on the lawn, art competitions and clowns' days. Check out the non-animal areas too – there is an inspirational Maasai exhibition with clothing, huts and artifacts, and an American Indian display with tipi and totem poles.

The play area is large and imaginative. It has lots of different areas for various aged children and includes a toddler tumble, an under-6's tumble room and a general play area with swinging and sliding devices for older children. It's busy during the school holidays, but with a customised tractor, fire engine and wooden houses to tempt it's not surprising. The indoor playbarn is great on a rainy day. Plus there are two mini trains giving trips around the park, although you may have to queue about 20 minutes to get on in busy periods.

☞ The Explorer Restaurant serves hot and cold food and has a number of different themed areas to choose from. Nearby is a restful and quiet garden, with live folk music when we went, plus loads of space for children to tire their legs out. There is a fast food cafe, ice-cream parlour and a picnic area too.

Several other attractions are dotted about, including a gift shop, the Teddy Safari shop, Drusilla's Pantry (home-made fudge), a bat exhibition and The Rainforest Story, an education area. Also look out for the 'paint and make' wacky workshops, which are an extra £1.00 per child. All in all, as about a third of the zoo is under cover, it is possible to go in wet weather.

When you've finished at Drusillas and fancy blowing away some cobwebs maybe, head south towards the sea from Drusillas. About 5 miles further on through the viallge of Alfriston itself, is the National Trust area of Frog Firle with great open views and downland walks.

Fact File

- ADDRESS: Drusillas Zoo Park, Alfriston, East Sussex
- TELEPHONE: 01323 870234
- WEBSITE: drusillas.co.uk
- DIRECTIONS: M23/A23, and then the A27 to Lewes. Follow the A27 on towards Polegate, and Drusillas is signposted off at the Wilmington roundabout
- PUBLIC TRANSPORT: Train to Polegate from Victoria, with a good taxi service from the station (3 miles)
- DISTANCE: 54 miles
- TRAVEL TIME: 1 hour 30 minutes
- OPENING: Daily from 10.00am-5.00pm (summer), or 4.00pm (winter)
- PRICES: Adults £7.60, children £6.50, under-3's free. Reduced rates in winter
- RESTAURANT FACILITIES: Yes
- NAPPY CHANGING FACILITIES: Yes
- HIGH CHAIRS: Yes
- DOGS: No
- PUSHCHAIR-FRIENDLY: Yes
- NEARBY: The South Downs, sea at Eastbourne or white cliffs at Beachy Head

Fishers Farm Park

THINK OF A PLACE WITH A REAL JAMBOREE OF ACTIVITIES FOR CHILDREN in a natural rural setting with farm animals alongside. That's Fishers Farm in a nutshell. To some extent the animals play second fiddle to the play zones, but a serious amount of thought has gone into laying on things for kids of all ages – and that even includes grown up kids! Combine it with a tranquil stroll in the grounds of nearby Petworth House at the end of the day and you are all sure to have a great day out. In the summer remember to bring towels and the children's swimsuits as there is a large pool they can splash about in.

You can pick up a plan of the Farm Park at the entrance, but will probably not need it as you'll find you will be dragged eagerly from pillar to post as the kids explore. Do take the timetable of events though as this gives the times of everything going on: not all activities run all day, so some planning and 'direction of operations' will be necessary. In particular, don't miss the Meet the Animals theatre events (twice a day), when farm animals are presented, you'll see a milking demonstration and your children may have a chance to go to the front of the audience and bottle feed a lamb.

> **"In the summer remember to bring towels and the children's swimsuits as there is a large pool"**

Walk through picturesque wooden barns at the start of the visit where a number of different beast are attractively housed: when we went there were goats, sheep, calves, small pigs and rabbits. You can get in with some of them for a bit of extra 'ooh-aah', though the lambs and kid goats were too tiny on our visit. We adults enjoyed the 1950's farm kitchen, but the kids raced on to the gipsy caravan resting alongside the horses at the end of the barn. As well as an enormous Shire horse and a very venerable mare, the ponies and tack used for pony rides outside can be inspected here. Both toddlers and older children are catered for on the pony rides, with hats provided, but you will probably have to queue and may not always get a ride.

If you don't manage to hone your equestrian skills there are plenty of other rides: namely the combine harvester, which was huge and something out of the ordinary, as well as a tractor and trailer ride. Our 2-year-old made a bee-line for the rows of real tractors and determinedly clambered up, until he noticed the merry-go-round which he then rode again and again (and again!). Meanwhile his siblings were off discovering wooden forts, assault courses, the helter skelter and climb-aboard boat in the extensive but well-contained adventure play areas. New attractions kept catching their eyes and the Park is nicely laid out in a series of different areas. Cross over the stream through the mini wild wood and you will find some sizeable trampolines and, possibly the biggest treat of all for our 7 and 8-year-olds, some fun go-carts. The nearby tuck shop sells some pretty mean doughnuts too.

In the summer an added attraction is the 'beach', an oversized paddling pool with sandy shore line. Just the thing on a hot day. Nearby is a massive sandpit too. There are lots of picnic tables dotted about so it is a good place to take a picnic. During school holidays additional theatre shows are put on, such as vets' talks and demonstrations, as well as magic tricks and clowns. Events vary throughout the year so you'll usually find something new for each visit. The shows are all indoors, and coupled with the indoor soft play areas near the restaurant at the entrance there is something to do even in the winter.

Fact File

- ADDRESS: Fishers Farm Park, Newpound Lane, Wisborough Green, W. Sussex
- TELEPHONE: Telephone: 01403 700063
- WEBSITE: www.fishersfarmpark.co.uk
- DIRECTIONS: A29 Dorking to Chichester Road, and A272 towards Wisborough Green. Turn off to the right, following signs, before the village
- PUBLIC TRANSPORT: None
- DISTANCE: 50 miles
- TRAVEL TIME: One hour 30 minutes
- OPENING: Daily 10.00am-5.00pm
- PRICES: Adults £7.75, children £6.75, family £26.00 (peak prices, less at other times)
- RESTAURANT FACILITIES: Yes
- NAPPY CHANGING FACILITIES: Yes
- HIGH CHAIRS: Yes
- DOGS: No
- PUSHCHAIR-FRIENDLY: Yes
- NEARBY: Follow the A272 further into Petworth and take a free walk in the peaceful and stunning grounds of Petworth House

Godstone Farm

*Tom, Tom the Piper's son,
stole a pig and away did run!*

NOT ONLY A SIZABLE FARM, BUT ALSO AN EPIC PLAY AREA FOR children, Godstone gives you the chance to really get out in the fields and blow away any cobwebs. Be warned though, it is deservedly popular, and queues to get into the car park on a busy summer's day have been known, so try going off season too.

The farm offers several attractions to plan your day around: a conventional farmyard with animal encounter pens, a wild walk through the woods and fields, and an extensive play area. Adding to the appeal is the way you keep coming across things unexpectedly, such as the forded stream in the duckery which our toddlers thought a great lark, especially as my son's wellies weren't quite high enough to prevent a bootfull! (He could have avoided this by crossing on the plank provided, but where's the fun in that?) I don't know who was more surprised during our picnic lunch, us or the sheep alongside, when to the accompaniment of piercing whistles we suddenly realised we were in the middle of a sheep dog demonstration.

> **"Plenty of opportunities for getting into the pens with different animals"**

We moved as quickly as is possible with three curious children through the incubator shed with their chicks and ducklings, past the 10-day-old Tamworth piglets (to cries of "Look, there's Curly!"), and on to the duckery and Marsh Walk. The duckery has several species of birds of which the crested ducks with their "funny haircuts" were much admired, as were the wooden bridges and ford.

Despite notices to the contrary the Marsh Walk is passable with a pushchair, if you don't mind getting very muddy wheels and lifting it over a couple of stiles at the end. The walk through the woods is well worth any effort though. It is an excitingly narrow, wet path (wellies essential), with plenty of streams and ponds for splashing in and loads of opportunities to get thoroughly muddy. Bring a jam jar at frog spawn time.

The Marsh Walk leads up to open fields and an upland barn, which is quiet and home to easily-viewed Shetland foals, goats and Highland calves. Next to the barn is the play area, so if little legs are getting tired with all the walking you have potential for a bit of bribery here.

Obviously built by a fanatic, the play area boasts a series of wooden constructions offering any number of bits to swing, balance, slide and clamber on. There are

tyres, wobbly walks, tunnels, a maze, bob sleighs, sand pits and tractors to scramble over, ranged across a huge hillside with fantastic views over the North Downs. Any pretence of keeping your children's clothes clean will have to be abandoned here – our little boy's speciality was cleaning slides with his backside. It has to be said that probably most of the equipment was designed for over-5's: it is fine for younger children on quiet days but at busy periods it may be hair-raising, and it would certainly be easy for them to disappear from view. There are picnic tables up here and a refreshment stall open at peak times.

Back in the farmyard there are plenty of opportunities for getting into the pens with different animals. There are goats, sheep, calves and pigs, as well as bees and a milking demonstration area. This part of the farm is particularly good for very young children; the rabbit pens were especially popular and there is an excellent indoor play area full of soft toys (50p extra charge – under 5's only). There is also a tea room with a sunny terrace overlooking a large sand pit with as many diggers and spades as small children could want. Perfect.

Fact File

● ADDRESS: Godstone Farm, Tilburstow Hill Road, Godstone, Surrey
● TELEPHONE: 01883 742546
● DIRECTIONS: A22 from junction 6 of the M25, to Godstone village. Signposted from the village
● PUBLIC TRANSPORT: Train to Redhill from Victoria. 410 bus to Godstone
● DISTANCE: 20 miles
● TRAVEL TIME: 45 minutes
● OPENING: Daily 10.00am-5.00pm
● PRICES: £3.80 per person over 2-years-old. One adult free with each paying child. Additional adults £3.80 each
● RESTAURANT FACILITIES: Yes
● NAPPY CHANGING FACILITIES: Yes
● HIGH CHAIRS: Yes
● DOGS: No
● PUSHCHAIR-FRIENDLY: Yes
● NEARBY: The Post Mill at Bletchingley, England's oldest working windmill and small agricultural museum (01342 843458)

Horton Park Children's Farm

DESPERATE FOR THE BLEAT OF A LAMB, OR THE SQUEAL OF A PIGLET? In the first bit of real open countryside as you leave south London, Horton Farm is a very quick and easy trip. All the usual farm animals are here to enjoy, there is plenty of space to picnic and run about and the added benefit of indoor facilities too. In 2000 a new indoor barn is opening.

From the entrance you go straight into a courtyard with various animals in pens around the outside: Longhorn cattle with amazingly-shaped horns; feathered-leg chickens looking as if they've got wellies on; and Angora goats with their soft woolly coats inviting you to bury your fingers in.

Further on are pigs, on the day we visited some had just farrowed and we peeked in at the three-day-old piglets with velvet ears. The kids could get a good look too by standing on the special supports giving small children a chance to see over the high sides. Next is the goat shed full of, unsurprisingly, goats, but also lambs, rabbits and piglets that you can get in with and stroke or prod. Excitement runs high for bottle-feeding the lambs

"Excitement runs high for bottle-feeding the lambs"

with children crowding round, their enthusiasm to have a go only exceeded by the lambs' readiness to grab the bottles. At other times of the year you can watch hand sheep-shearing, cuddle newborn chicks and ducklings, or feed kid goats.

Alongside the goats is another large barn, when we were there full of pregnant and nursing ewes. We said "aah" at the new born lambs and sympathised with the ewes huffing and puffing with their enormous swollen bellies. If we'd stood around long enough I think we would have seen a lamb being born. Later on in the year this 'maternity suite' holds goats and kids, horses and foals, or more pigs and piglets so you will always be able to catch some baby animals.

Outside you can follow a track around to visit all the animals in open runs in the fields: ducks, turkeys and geese in the winter, plus pigs, goats and cattle when the weather is warmer. In summertime you can take tractor rides around the farm for an additional 50p per person. The outdoor playground is quite large with enough wobble

and scramble activities to keep adventurous children busy for some time, whilst you sit and relax (well, maybe). Our cowboys and indians stormed the wooden fort before scooting off to be tigers climbing the jungle. There is a small shop selling ices there in the summer, some picnic tables and a bigger picnic area in an orchard next to the courtyard. There is a further play area for older kids, a wooden maze in the copse too, and, so that no one feels neglected, there is an area set aside for under-6's with ride-on tractors and cars.

Children can live it up in the straw pit and all around you'll see straw-speckled children: a highlight of the day with our rowdy crew. It's under cover, making it a good place to warm up or retreat to in damp weather. Next door is another picnic area and a large wooden adventure castle, both undercover too. The tearooms by the main farm building are open all year.

The adjacent Horton Country Park (01327 732466) is good for a stroll, with well-tended all-weather paths taking you past the riding school (lots of horses) to open fields, woods, ponds and so on. All in all, an unexpected taste of the country, right on the edge of the city.

Fact File

● ADDRESS: Horton Park Children's Farm, Horton Lane, Epsom, Surrey
● TELEPHONE: 01372 743984
● DIRECTIONS: Follow directions to Chessington World of Adventure from A3 (the A243) or M25 (junction 9). Turn off A243 at Malden Rushett traffic lights into Rushett Lane towards Epsom, left at new roundabout and follow signs to farm
● PUBLIC TRANSPORT: Bus from Epsom
● DISTANCE: 20 miles
● TRAVEL TIME: 30 minutes
● OPENING: Daily 10.00am-6.00pm (summer), or 5.00pm (winter)
● PRICES: £3.65 per person over 2-years-old. One adult free with each paying child. Under-2's free
● RESTAURANT FACILITIES: Yes
● NAPPY CHANGING FACILITIES: Yes
● HIGH CHAIRS: Yes
● DOGS: No
● PUSHCHAIR-FRIENDLY: Yes
● NEARBY: Epsom Common, back along Christchurch Road, where you can walk to the Stew Pond and Great Pond, both full of wildlife

Odds Farm Park

THIS IS A SMALL, FRIENDLY FARM AND RARE BREEDS CENTRE WITH plenty of healthy happy animals. It is close to London, an easy drive, and with a mix of indoor and outdoor areas, it is perfect to visit even if the weather is poor.

As we went in we were met by lambs and calves in the barn by the entrance. Looking like a nativity scene, it was an immediate hit because we had arrived at calf-feeding time and the children were able to assist with bottle-feeding the calves, much to their delight. The green-sweatshirted staff, friendly and kind everywhere, were particularly helpful here as they explained what was going on.

The Farm offers plenty of these hands-on opportunities: bottle-feeding the lambs, hand-milking the goats, egg collecting and feeding the pigs. Many of these are seasonal, and will vary from visit to visit, so there is always something new for children to try. Look out for the timetable of feeding/handling times at the entrance and plan your day around the special activities.

Our daughter was obsessed by the long-haired and long-eared rabbits in the pet handling area. Have your reasons for not buying rabbits ready, as they are very adorable and for sale. We spent ages in there and just managed to get out without buying at least a dozen! In addition, there is a special enclosed 'Pat-a-pet' area with limited opening periods in the walk through barn and, also under cover, you can see lambing in the new 'poly-tunnel'.

"Babies can get a good view of everything from a buggy"

Outside in the paddocks, the path winds round enclosures for curly-haired Jacobs sheep and dreadlocked Wensleydales, goats with unbelievable horns, cows and donkeys. They all look fantastic. There are pigs with litters of piglets wallowing in mud too. When we were there these piglets were very friendly, nuzzling up to the fence and clambering all over each other. I'm not sure who squealed the most: them or the children, but there was much excitement all round.

There are plenty of notices explaining the breeds as you go around, which is just as well, as some of them are very unfamiliar. Be prepared to identify a Spangled Humbug Miniature or a Buff Orpington (clue – they are both breeds of chicken). Babies can get a good view of everything from a buggy. One enclosure is open for feeding and handling opportunities, and you can take a pushchair in there too.

The grassy adventure playground and picnic area are a real treat. Set right in the middle, so you can see everything going on, they are perfect in the summer. The playground has wooden play equipment, plus a separate under-5's section and sand pit with toys. Picnic tables and chairs are provided.

There is a toy tractor track too, which is outside in the summer. The rest of the year it is in an indoor play area, with hay bales, old tyres, tractors and trikes too. Nearby are the tearooms, so you can have a cup of tea whilst the youngsters practise their stunts. For those who like the real thing, there's a 20-minute tractor trailer ride round the farm park for a small extra charge.

The gift shop has the usual farm stuff plus local produce, jams, pickles and so on. We particularly liked the thoughtfully-provided Brio railtrack to keep little fingers occupied! Similar diversions are given in the tearooms, which are overlooking the animals and have toys and colouring materials on hand.

Finally, do look out for the special events. For a small extra charge themed activities and children's crafts are often on offer.

Fact File

● ADDRESS: Odds Farm Park Rare Breeds Centre, Wooburn Common, High Wycombe, Buckinghamshire
● TELEPHONE: 01628 520188
● WEBSITE: www.oddsfarm.co.uk
● DIRECTIONS: M40 junction 2. Follow the A40 in the High Wycombe direction for nearly 2 miles, then turn left into Broad Lane and go a mile further. The farm is second on the left, just after the pub
● PUBLIC TRANSPORT: Beaconsfield train station (trains from Marylebone) 4-mile taxi ride
● DISTANCE: 25 miles
● TRAVEL TIME: 45 minutes
● OPENING: 10.00am-5.00pm daily mid February to end of October. 10.00-4.00pm Thursday to Sunday during the rest of the year
● PRICES: Adults £3.95, children £2.95, under-2's free
● RESTAURANT FACILITIES: Yes
● NAPPY CHANGING FACILITIES: Yes
● HIGH CHAIRS: Yes
● DOGS: No
● PUSHCHAIR-FRIENDLY: Yes
● NEARBY: Burnham Beeches, or the beautiful National Trust grounds of Cliveden Hotel (01628 605069)

Wimpole Home Farm

FOR WAGONS, PIGS AND TRACTORS COME TO WIMPOLE. THIS beautifully-restored late Georgian farm is owned by the National Trust and lies in the grounds of one of their properties, Wimpole Hall. For adults it offers a fascinating view of the way farms used to be, although I suspect a lot cleaner than in reality, whilst for children there are plenty of animals and farm vehicles to admire.

Stroll down to the Farm from the main Hall. It takes about 10 minutes and goes through the 1790's pleasure garden. Coming into the farm you are immediately struck by the smell of good old farmyard manure, and hordes of squawking, flapping geese and chickens. The usual fun can be had by children admiring them (well, chasing, actually). The farm is laid out around a traditional yard, with rare breeds of cattle in the centre, and other animals in the surrounding barns and sheds. These handsome buildings are all wooden and several have thatched roofs.

The children will be more impressed by the animals: rare breeds of pigs, goats, and horses. There were no less than three litters of piglets when we visited, so there was much excitement

"Good old farmyard manure, and hordes of squawking, flapping geese and chickens"

(from all parties)! The pens are all arranged so that even toddlers can get a good view, except for the Shire horse who was unsociably hidden away in his stable on our visit.

There is a wagon museum full of restored painted wagons, barrows and carts. They give a romantic glimpse of rural life in the late eighteenth and nineteenth centuries – you can almost hear the dancing round the Maypole. Meanwhile, the interactive farm museum in the old barn gives a nice history of the farm, for adults, whilst children can enjoy trying on the costumes and

building with beams.

Other attractions include a rabbit barn, a short walk past fields of sheep and goats, a wooden adventure play area in the woods, and a play area with real and toy tractors, surrounded by picnic tables. There is also a duck pond – suitably green and slimy – with picnic tables adjacent too.

There are toilets down at the Farm, a shop, and a restaurant in one of the barns. Facilities can also be found back up in the stableblock and main Hall.

Don't miss the Hall grounds and gardens. They are

very extensive, consisting of lovely Capability Brown wooded parkland, with mature trees, woodland, a folly, bridges and lakes. Entry to the park is free and you can picnic at will. There are several waymarked walks through the park, ranging in length. Pick up a walks leaflet in the stableblock (£1.00). The walk down to the lower lake and beyond to the folly gives lovely views back to the Hall.

There are several special events throughout the year at both the farm and Hall. Look out for the lambing weekends at the farm in March, and costume fairs, craft fairs, classic car rallies and children's fun days held throughout the year.

Fact File

- ● ADDRESS: Wimpole Hall & Home Farm, Arrington, Royston, Hertfordshire
- ● TELEPHONE: 01223 207257
- ● WEBSITE: www.nationaltrust.org.uk
- ● DIRECTIONS: Off the A603, 8 miles SW of Cambridge. Follow the Wimpole Hall sign from the A11 or A1198 junction with the A603
- ● PUBLIC TRANSPORT: Nearest train station is 5 miles away at Shepreth
- ● DISTANCE: 55 miles
- ● TRAVEL TIME: 1 hour 30 minutes
- ● OPENING: 10.30am-5.00pm from 18 March to 31 October, every day except Mondays and Fridays (but including Bank Holidays June to August). Open weekends 11.00am-4.00pm in the winter
- ● PRICES: Adults £4.70 adults, children £2.70, under-3's free. Combined ticket with Hall available. Reduced prices for National Trust members
- ● RESTAURANT FACILITIES: Yes
- ● NAPPY CHANGING FACILITIES: Yes
- ● HIGH CHAIRS: Yes
- ● DOGS: No
- ● PUSHCHAIR-FRIENDLY: Yes
- ● NEARBY: RSPB bird sanctuary at Sandy (01767 680551)

Woodside Farm & Wild Fowl Park

You will be surprised at both the scale and the comprehensive nature of the facilities at Woodside. However, it's compact with a good mix of indoor and outdoor facilities and so is a great place to go on those days when you're not quite sure whether it's going to rain or shine.

We visited on a Monday when it was very quiet with a few other toddler and carer groups pottering around like us. Because it was so quiet we had the impression that the whole enterprise was staffed by about three people who kept dashing from coffee shop to farm shop to attractions as their customers moved around: this didn't matter in the least as no-one was in a great hurry but did add to our amusement!

Woodside is set in just over six acres of woodland and feels very extensive, despite a three-hour stay we didn't get all the way round. This was partly because our children were diverted by the play area with its 'Tarzan Trail' which kept them busy for a good half an hour enabling us to catch up on conversation as we watched from the picnic table.

There are over 150 species of farm animals and wildfowl here. Punnets of food are on sale at the entrance. As far as animals are concerned the two big hits for us were firstly James, an extremely hungry goat, and secondly the pigs wallowing in some glorious mud which of course meant that the children had to share in the experience and get as muddy as possible! There is a large indoor area where children can get in and handle rabbits and guinea pigs, and feed the likes of sheep, goats and lambs.

"You can collect the eggs yourselves to take home"

A huge range of different poultry and wildfowl are kept in grassy enclosures and alongside various ponds. Children can feed the birds too. Apart from poultry and wildfowl, you'll see lots of owls in an aviary, and storks, cranes and flamingos daintily balancing in three new ponds. There is a barn egg grading and packing display in a large barn and you can collect the free-range eggs yourselves to take home priced 85p a half-dozen.

A tractor trailer ride round the site is laid on each day, at a small extra cost (70p per person), and at weekends and throughout the school holidays there are also pony rides, charged at £1.00. Hats are provided and there are various sized ponies for all ages of children. There are

☞ loads of events going on – reptile celebrities, Punch and Judy or Magic shows, and Easter Egg hunts to name but a few. Most weeks you will find something new happening. From the end of May there are even some monkies arriving!

All of the layout, range of animals, style of presentation and upkeep of the farm are impressive and make it an easy day out for grown ups with no chance for children to get bored. The coffee shop offers sandwiches and hot food although you'll need the second door opening if you arrive with a double buggy otherwise you won't get in. There are also lots of picnic areas, both indoors and outside.

Fact File

● ADDRESS: Woodside Farm Shop and Wild Fowl Park, Mancroft Road, Slip End, Luton, Bedfordshire
● TELEPHONE: 01582 841044
● WEBSITE: www.woodsidefarm.co.uk
● DIRECTIONS: Take the A5 towards Dunstable from the M1 junction 9. Turn right after 2 miles, onto the B4540 to Luton, following the brown tourist signs to the farm
● PUBLIC TRANSPORT: Train to Luton, then short taxi ride (about £2.50)
● DISTANCE: 35 miles
● TRAVEL TIME: 1 hour
● OPENING: Monday to Saturday 8.00am-5.30pm all year
● PRICES: Adults £2.50, children £1.90, babies under 6 months free
● RESTAURANT FACILITIES: Yes
● NAPPY CHANGING FACILITIES: Yes
● HIGH CHAIRS: Yes
● DOGS: No
● PUSHCHAIR-FRIENDLY: Yes
● NEARBY: Stockwood Country Park in Luton has a craft museum, and the Mossman collection of horse-drawn vehicles, with daily rides through the park

Look! Look! Look!

Barleylands Farm Museum

HEAVEN FOR TRACTOR FANATICS, BARLEYLANDS HAS OVER 50 tractors centre stage in a compact museum. During the summer the collection of steam traction engines are operational, there is a miniature railway and the chance to pick your own strawberries, so there is always plenty to see and do.

The museum itself is devoted to farm equipment and machinery and is housed in a series of barns set around a pretty little courtyard. There are tractors, tractors and more tractors: splendid bright red, orange, green and blue ones, and we had considerable debate over which colour was the nicest. Old ones, newer ones, big and small ones, and even radio-controlled ones: there is no shortage of them to feast your eyes on. The museum is also stuffed full of other bits of old farm tools, mostly labelled so you

"See the tractors doing their stuff: huffing and puffing, heaving and clanking around in the big fields"

can have fun going round trying to work out what everything could have been used for before checking your answers. Do be careful to keep an eye on your kids though, as the bits and pieces are all genuine farm machinery, and could be dangerous if kids mucked about with them. That being said there didn't seem much harm in the odd clamber up to wiggle the gears and steering wheel, and no-one seemed to mind.

Outside the barns are the really big beasts, including vintage steam-powered ones. From Easter onwards, you can often see these doing their stuff at weekends: huffing and puffing, heaving and clanking around in the big fields out to the back of the museum. Even if they are not operational on the day you visit, they are still pretty impressive. Tractor and trailer rides are sometimes available too.

You'll find a miniature railway at the rear of the museum. This runs on Sundays and Bank Holidays from March to October (daily in August), and takes you for a 15-minute jaunt across the fields for about £1.00 per person. It is worth doing as it takes you down to the farm shop and fruit picking area. During the summer there is something on every Sunday: guided farm tours, bread-making demonstrations, rural life displays and childrens' activities.

Strawberry picking with children is great fun: the rules are simple – you only pick the red ones – and there is always the possibility of finding the Biggest Best Strawberry Ever. Take your own containers, or use the ones available at the farm shop, but make sure you have plenty of recipes as you will always come back with more than you bargained for. Other soft fruit and vegetables are also available.

You can have a pleasant little walk back along the farm trail once you've picked your fill. Try out the wooden play area for size while you are there. Back next to the museum there is an animal petting area with calves and rabbits, as well as a noisy collection of crowing cockerels, bleating goats and snorting pigs who inhabit the inner courtyard. Bags of food are available at the entrance for 25p. New in 2000 is a chick hatchery.

Have a look at the glassworks. There is a viewing gallery so you can see the stuff being made, with a small shop selling glassware alongside. Our kids were fascinated. There is also a working blacksmith, and several different craft studios demonstrating and selling craftworks.

Try the new tearoom which is good for families. An alternative is to bring a picnic and eat out on the grass or there are tables in the courtyard, so bring some cream for those strawberries! You can use the lecture room next to the glassworks in wet weather.

Barleylands is renowned in the area for its Steam Rally and Country Show, usually held the second weekend in September. If you come then you'll be entertained with all sorts of working craft stalls – blacksmiths, wheelwrights and coopers to name a few – steam fairground rides and heaps of working steam engines. During the rest of the season there are other events too, so just ring to check in advance.

Fact File

● ADDRESS: Barleylands Farm, Barleylands Road, Billericay, Essex
● TELEPHONE: 01268 532253
● DIRECTIONS: A12 out of London, and pick up the A127 Southend road. Follow signposts to farm museum just before Basildon
● PUBLIC TRANSPORT: None
● DISTANCE: 35 miles
● TRAVEL TIME: 1 hour 15 minutes
● OPENING: 10.00am-5.00pm, daily from beginning of March to end of October
● PRICES: Adults £3.25, children £1.75, under-3's free
● RESTAURANT FACILITIES: Yes
● NAPPY CHANGING FACILITIES: Yes
● HIGH CHAIRS: Yes
● DOGS: Yes
● PUSHCHAIR-FRIENDLY: Yes
● NEARBY: Southend on Sea for pier, funfair, beach and kiss-me-quick type fun

Bekonscot Model Village

STEP BACK INTO THE 1930'S ENGLAND OF AGATHA CHRISTIE AND visit this charming and intricate model village. The tidy world-in-miniature has efficient trains chugging about, cars with running boards, village corner shops and pubs, and wholesome, cheerful model people. The detail is superb, with a lot of humorous touches for adults, whilst there are a wealth of tiny features to amuse and fascinate children. Thoughtfully provided with picnic spots and an adventure playground too, Bekonscot makes an easy, fun day out with something for everyone. However, it is very popular in August, and can get crowded then, also attracting many wasps. In the summer term there are often school visits in the morning, so it is best to time your arrival afterwards.

The village is set in one and a half acres of garden, and has over 170 buildings. A microcosm of idealised rural and village life is represented: shops (even a 1950's M & S), churches, schools, castles, and with a zoo, fishing harbour, fairground and racecourse, to name just a few of the features.

"With several stations, lots of tunnels, viaducts and bridges, trains seem to keep popping-up everywhere"

Recent additions are are a Tudor showhouse, hop garden, thatched cottage (on fire) and airport. See if you can find them all! A sinewy, narrow path snakes in and out, up and down through the village and surrounding 'countryside', providing good variety and the chance to see all the detail well, particularly for children, as much is at their level.

It took us about an hour to go all the way round once. You have to follow the path and set route through, and some passing places are provided. You may get held up at busy times, however, you can go round and round as many times as you like. The path is easily passable with a single buggy, but a double buggy would get stuck in places (although tandem style ones would manage it).

A model railway with five trains busily runs around covering more or less the whole site. With several stations, lots of tunnels, viaducts and bridges, trains seem to keep popping-up everywhere. You can even see inside the life-sized signal box, where the signalman controls the points and signals with levers, just like a real railway.

No village is complete without its babbling brook. The little stream here merrily runs through part of the village, passing over a water wheel attached to a mill, and down over a waterfall into the 'sea', which, complete with pier, fishing harbour and lighthouse, is one of the most attractive features of the village. (If you wonder why wires run over the water, they are to discourage herons landing to make a meal of the huge carp lurking underwater.)

The garden that the village is laid in is wonderfully designed and maintained, and has lots of lovely miniature

☞ trees and shrubs, as well as a host of rockery plants and flowers. In the spring and summer the gardens are beautiful. There are full-sized trees too, with benches around, which provide welcome resting points in the shade for the footsore.

There are lots of picnic tables and benches in one corner of the garden. The refreshment kiosk is at the far end of the village, selling pizzas, burgers and hot dogs, as well as sandwiches, snacks, ices and teas. You can sit on tables and benches at the picnic area near the kiosk, but there is no inside seating there. However, there is a greenhouse near the main entrance with tables and seats, and you can sit there in wet or cold weather.

The adventure playground has good slides and climbing castles, with seating for adults. It's not huge, and may be hectic sometimes.

A shop at the entrance, located in an old railway carriage, has a small range of small toys and gifts.

Fact File

● ADDRESS: Bekonscot Model Village, Warwick Road, Beaconsfield, Buckinghamshire
● TELEPHONE: 01494 672919
● WEBSITE: www.bekonscot.org.uk
● DIRECTIONS: M40, leaving at Junction 2, signposted for Beaconsfield and The Model Village. Follow signs. Bekonscot is off a side road behind Waitrose in Beaconsfield New village
● PUBLIC TRANSPORT: Train from Marylebone to Beaconsfield (10-minute walk)
● DISTANCE: 30 miles
● TRAVEL TIME: 1 hour
● OPENING: Daily 10.00am-5.00pm from 19 February to 29 October
● PRICES: Adults £4.50, children £2.50, under-3's free, family £12.00
● RESTAURANT FACILITIES: Limited
● NAPPY CHANGING FACILITIES: Yes
● HIGH CHAIRS: No
● DOGS: No
● PUSHCHAIR-FRIENDLY: Yes
● NEARBY: Wycombe Airfield (01494 529261), near High Wycombe, with restaurant and picnic area, and where you can see small planes, helicopters and gliders busying about

Bentley Wildfowl & Motor Museum

There once was an ugly duckling . . .

WITH A WINNING COMBINATION OF VINTAGE CARS AND WATERFOWL, Bentley is sure to appeal to most families. Set in an elegant country estate, deep in the Sussex countryside, it offers plenty for a good day out. From 2000 there is a new reed bed ecology area with natural wild life and hides.

Depending on the weather, it is probably best to start with the birds. This gives you the chance to get rid of the bags of birdfood that your children will have persuaded you to buy at the entrance for 25p a bag. The birds are all kept in a large series of enclosures, with wide pushchair-friendly paths. Some paths can be slightly muddy in places – especially after periods of wet weather. There is a lot of open water, and although most of it is fenced you will need to be a bit careful with toddlers. There is

"Collect an identification chart at the entrance and children will love spotting all the varieties"

a choice of three routes around the enclosures – taking 30, 45 or 60 minutes. Each route leads you through part of the collection: there are over 1,000 swans, geese and ducks which can be readily seen and appreciated.

Designed with close contact between birds and visitors in mind, there are plenty of opportunities for both adults and children to see the birds at close quarters, especially if you have food for them. Collect an identification chart at the entrance and children will love spotting all the different varieties.

The motor museum should appeal to all car-freaks, large and small. The collection is very impressive. It is under cover and ranges from a 1960's bubble car (when did you last see one of those?), through gleaming Ferrari and Aston Martin sports numbers, to dinky-toy-like Vintage cars and bicycles. Children are not allowed to climb on the cars. Next to it, though, is an education area with a woodland theme and plenty of hands-on opportunities.

Outside again, the grounds have several further attractions. There is a woodland trail which takes about half an hour, and is resplendent in spring and summer with daffodils and bluebells. This may be passable in the summer with a pushchair, but when we went it was too muddy.

A miniature steam train offers short rides for 40p per person, taking you up to the woods, with a short circuit in front of the woods, and a second station there. It runs at weekends April to September, and Wednesdays and Bank Holiday Mondays too in August. There is also a good adventure playground and a small farm.

Food and drinks are available in the small, pleasant tearoom and there are tables in the courtyard too, if you want to sit outside. The tearoom has light lunches, as well as teas and cakes. There is only one high chair. However, the extensive grassy grounds offer plenty of potential picnic spots. Finally, there are always some resident craftspeople doing their thing, amongst which you should find glass sculpting, wood carving, spinning and weaving to admire.

Fact File

- ADDRESS: Bentley Wildfowl & Motor Museum, Halland, East Sussex
- TELEPHONE: 01825 840573
- WEBSITE: www.bentley.org.uk
- DIRECTIONS: From the M25 take the A22 south to East Grinstead and on towards Eastbourne. Beyond Uckfield look for a brown sign off the A22, and after about 3 miles follow white signs to Bentley
- PUBLIC TRANSPORT: None
- DISTANCE: 50 miles
- TRAVEL TIME: 1 hour 30 minutes
- OPENING: Daily from 20 March to 31 October 10.30am-4.30pm. Weekends only in February, rest of March and November
- PRICES: Adults £4.80, children £3.00, under-4's free. Family ticket £14.50. Reduced rates in winter
- RESTAURANT FACILITIES: Yes
- NAPPY CHANGING FACILITIES: Yes
- HIGH CHAIRS: Yes
- DOGS: No
- PUSHCHAIR-FRIENDLY: Yes
- NEARBY: Barkham Manor Vineyard offers wine tasting, vineyard trail, picnic site and tours of winery (01825 722103)

Birdworld

FOR BIRD-LOVERS, BIRDWORLD IS A MUST. IT'S A STIMULATING AND unusual day out, amidst beautiful garden surroundings. Really a zoo for birds, it has all sorts of different species – colourful and otherwise – on display and displaying themselves in enclosures and cages. Handling potential of the birds themselves is limited, but there is plenty to see and listen to, and feathers to collect. There are opportunities to handle some animals in a separate small farm area and a short road train ride in the summer too.

The cages and enclosures are well set-out along paths which are easily negotiable with pushchairs. Some enclosures have hedging round them which can be a bit high for very small children to see over, although there are often holes in the hedge for peering through. However, most of the birds can readily be seen, especially those in the cages. Some, like the ostrich, are quite friendly, so you can see them at close quarters.

There are birds from all over the world. Highlights are the noisy, squawking parrots with their bright plumage, the laughing ducks, flamingos and pelicans on the lake, and, of course,

Penguin Island. This is home to about 30 penguins and has a very good underwater viewing enclosure, which lets you see the birds diving and playing underwater. Penguin feeding at 11.30am and 3.30pm is great fun. Book in advance to feed them yourself and the £5.00 charge is donated to charity (over-5's only).

Other special features include the seashore walk with terns and oyster catchers amidst waves and a fishing boat, the parrots-in-flight aviary, and the tropical walk which has exotic birds in a heated environment. Our children were fascinated by the egg collection; ranging from the tiny yellow woodpecker's egg looking like a mint imperial to the colossal ostrich's. If you catch the 30-minute talks in the Heron theatre, you'll get a chance to learn more and see several Birdworld inhabitants appearing in starring roles (1.00pm and 3.00pm, plus additional ones in the summer).

"Plenty to see, listen to, and feathers to collect"

Jenny Wren farm will appeal to children; with its clutch of farm animals, some roaming around freely. There are set handling times throughout the day when you can get to know the animals. You'll find a play area down at the farm too.

The free road train ride is a 10-minute round trip, running weekends from April, daily in the Easter holidays, and daily from the beginning of June. The station is by the good children's playground, which has slides, swings and climbing paraphernalia alongside a picnic area with tables, benches and a cafe. More snacks and loos can be found at Jenny Wren Farm, whilst larger facilities and the gift shop are at the entrance.

Adjacent to the Birdworld entrance is Underwater World which houses a small display of freshwater and marine fish and which can be a good refuge in wet weather. The latest attraction there is crocodiles!

There are Fundays planned during the spring and summer, when entertainment, games and competitions are laid-on throughout the day. Telephone in advance to get details.

Fact File

- ADDRESS: Birdworld, Holt Pound, Farnham, Surrey
- TELEPHONE: 01420 22140
- WEBSITE: www.birdworld.co.uk
- DIRECTIONS: A3 to Guildford, and then the A31 (Hogs Back) to Farnham. Signposted from the end of the Hogs Back dual carriageway. Alternatively, signposted from junction 4 of the M3
- PUBLIC TRANSPORT: Train from Waterloo to Aldershot (6-mile bus ride), Farnham (3-mile taxi ride) or Bentley (30-minute signposted walk through forest)
- DISTANCE: 40 miles
- TRAVEL TIME: 1 hour 15 minutes
- OPENING: Daily, February to end October and December, 9.30am-4.30pm (summer) or 3.30pm (winter). Weekends only November and January
- PRICES: Adults £7.95, children £4.75, under-3's free, family £22.95
- RESTAURANT FACILITIES: Yes
- NAPPY CHANGING FACILITIES: Yes
- HIGH CHAIRS: Yes
- DOGS: No
- PUSHCHAIR-FRIENDLY: Yes
- NEARBY: Birdworld is set in the Alice Holt forest, which has trails and picnic areas suitable for pushchairs. Near to Frensham Ponds

Brighton Sea Life Centre

BRIGHTON IS ALWAYS A FUN PLACE TO VISIT WITH YOUNG CHILDREN – the sea, a grand pier to stroll along, the maze of little shops in the Lanes area behind the sea front, or the delightful park next to the Pavilion buildings. The Sea Life Centre, next to the pier, is completely indoors and means that Brighton is still a good trip even in wet or cold weather.

If you and your children are not completely fazed by practically rubbing noses with a shark or tickling a sting-ray, then you will have a wonderful time. Start by walking through the series of sea and freshwater aquariums in the elegantly restored Victorian display area. Huge fish glide inches away in floor to ceiling tanks, which are subtly-lit and ingeniously modelled to re-create underwater scenes. Wrecks, sunken treasure and ominous caverns abound. The size of the tanks and the viewing platforms means that children (even those in pushchairs) get a really good view.

"Feeding of the denizens of the deep takes place twice a day"

These displays open out to a wider area, where a sandy sea-bed has been re-created on one side, and an old harbour the other. The sandy sea-bed is teeming with graceful sting-rays, which rear up out of the water to say hello. For the brave there are instructions given on how to stroke the rays: apparently they are very gentle and don't sting unless you tread on them (so don't get *in* the tank . .)! If you want your children to touch the rays you have to lift them up to do it. Food for the rays is on sale nearby, so you can even feed them if you want.

The old harbour is full of creaking boards and sounds of seagulls, with plenty of huge crabs dancing over the sea-bed. You can get to meet these at close quarters in

the Touch Pool talks, where there are opportunities to handle starfish and crabs. Walk on through more tanks displaying deep-water creatures, such as octopus and lobsters. Some of these tanks have special viewing bubbles, enabling you to feel that you are in the water with the beasties! Particularly engrossing is the Kingdom of the Sea Horse display where you can see native sea horses, bred in captivity, and their cousins from all over the world.

The underwater tunnel is most impressive. With its shipwreck-theme entrance it offers superb close-up views of British sharks, more sting-rays and conger eels. Feeding time does not leave much to the imagination, and much excitement will be had as these mysterious animals glide and cavort above your heads. There is an underwater camera which allows you to zoom in yourself as if you are really swimming in there with them. Go up to the opened top of the shark tank to the Jules Verne themed auditorium for talks and feeding displays.

The sharks are fed every other day, but if you miss this, feeding of other denizens of the deep takes placed twice a day – piranas and tropical fish in particular.

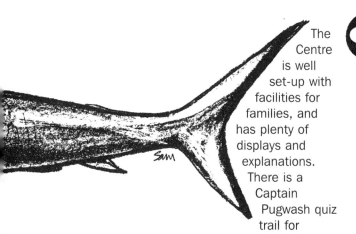

The Centre is well set-up with facilities for families, and has plenty of displays and explanations. There is a Captain Pugwash quiz trail for primary-aged kids, and a soft play area for younger ones. Access with a pushchair is best via the side entrance leading off the seafront, with no steps to negotiate at all.

Finally, your admission ticket is valid all day, so you can pop back in after a stroll along the Front with your fish and chips!

Fact File

- ADDRESS: Brighton Sea Life Centre, Marine Parade, Brighton, East Sussex
- TELEPHONE: 01273 604233
- WEBSITE: www.sealife.co.uk
- DIRECTIONS: M23 and A23 straight to Brighton and head for the sea front
- PUBLIC TRANSPORT: Frequent train services from Victoria station. Brighton station is a 15-minute walk from the Centre
- DISTANCE: 50 miles
- TRAVEL TIME: 1 hour 30 minutes
- OPENING: 10.00am-4.00pm daily, later in summer
- PRICES: Adults £5.95, children £3.95, under-4's free
- RESTAURANT FACILITIES: Yes
- NAPPY CHANGING FACILITIES: Yes
- HIGH CHAIRS: Yes
- DOGS: No
- PUSHCHAIR-FRIENDLY: Yes
- NEARBY: Sussex Toy and Model Museum (01273 749494), next to the train station, or Pirates Deep (01273 674549) an indoor play area open weekends, and daily in the school holidays

Cotswold Wildlife Park

COME HERE TO SEE WILD ANIMALS THAT YOU CAN'T SEE ON A FARM — real lions, rhinos and zebras to name a few, in 120 acres of gardens and landscaped parkland around a large Gothic-style manor house. It offers a varied, exciting day out and is just as much fun in winter as summer.

On arrival we headed straight for the real wild animals: the leopards, lions and rhinos. Well-signposted paths radiate out from the car park, so you can easily work out which way to go. On the way we admired the giant tortoises: huge boulders which unexpectedly started walking towards us. Despite wanting to ride on them, our daughter was tempted away with promises of more to come.

After a short walk past a vast, empty field we came to the zebra house, leopard house, and most spectacularly the lions. Obviously zebras and leopards aren't stupid (it was a cold day) as they were all inside, but the large glass windows in their houses, with steps up for children, meant we could all get a wonderful view of them. The lions were prowling around looking highly ferocious, but the close up sight of those sharp

"The lions were prowling around outside looking highly ferocious"

yellow teeth, glinting eyes and huge paws (even safely behind wire netting) proved too much for our daughter and we had to beat a hasty retreat to the relative safety of the Bactrian camels.

Back around the manor house there are plenty more animals to see – red pandas, monkeys, gibbons and emus are just some of what is on offer. They are all well-displayed, with ditches and viewing platforms enabling you to get a really close-up look. To be within six foot of a white rhino is quite an experience and our son was clearly enthralled, although we were not able to persuade him that it wasn't a "dawg"! There is also a children's farmyard area, with a good display of pot-bellied pigs, angora goats, rabbits, guinea pigs, ducks and poultry. Some of these may be stroked and petted, and they are all accessible for small children to see and appreciate.

The manor house and attached buildings contain a number of other attractions, including the reptile and invertebrate houses. Warm, with subdued lighting and suitably impressive slimies and slitheries, these proved very popular, although children have to be lifted to see inside some displays. The bat house, where you can look down on the bats swirling below you, was fascinating. It adjoins the glass animal house, where you can see a myriad of miniature glass animals both on display and being made.

Other areas to visit are the walled garden with otters, meerkats, penguins, and hornbills. Many more birds, including flamingos, cranes, swans and ducks can be seen in the lake area. You may not feed them though. All the paths are easily accessible to pushchairs, including those round the lake, and there are plenty of good, clear information boards and signs.

Behind the manor house you'll find an adventure playground with slides, swings, climbing equipment and other amusements for children from babyhood to at least eight-years-old. The helter-skelter is quite awe-inspiring and very popular with five-year-olds. The playground may get crowded in busy periods.

There is also a narrow gauge railway which runs at 20-minute intervals and takes you on a short tour of the whole park past most of the animals' enclosures (£1.00 adults, 50p children).

The park is well-served with picnic areas, with a large picnic lawn in front of the manor house, and picnic tables in several other locations, including the adventure playground. There is a large self-service cafe, with a highly distracting baby dinosaur display (lizards to you and me). Half of the seating area is non-smoking.

During the summer there are many special events, including birds of prey flying demonstrations, car rallies and snake handling days (first Sunday in the month from June to September).

Fact File

- ADDRESS: Cotswold Wildlife Park, Burford, Oxfordshire
- TELEPHONE: 01993 823006
- DIRECTIONS: M40 to junction 8, around the Oxford ring road and take the A40 to Burford. Signposted off the A361 from Burford
- PUBLIC TRANSPORT: None
- DISTANCE: 60 miles
- TRAVEL TIME: 1 hour 30 minutes
- OPENING: Daily 10.00am-5.00pm or dusk, whichever earlier
- PRICES: £5.80 adults, £3.80 children, under-3's free
- RESTAURANT FACILITIES: Yes
- NAPPY CHANGING FACILITIES: Yes
- HIGH CHAIRS: Yes
- DOGS: Yes
- PUSHCHAIR-FRIENDLY: Yes
- NEARBY: Cotswolds Motor Museum (01451 821255) or Model Village (01451 820467) at Bourton-On-The-Water

Didcot Railway Centre

Aye, man and boy, my father too, and his father before him . . .

GRAB YOUR THERMOS, DON YOUR ANORAK AND SET OFF FOR A DAY IN homage to God's Wonderful Railway (GWR, the Great Western Railway) at Didcot. Here you can marvel at some of the heaviest and strongest steam engines ever built. Move over Thomas – here comes the 3288! If you think you've had enough of steam engine romanticism, think again – this one is not to be missed.

Didcot was a centre of operations for the Great Western Railway from its heyday at the early part of this century through to its closure in the mid 1960's. Now a museum of those golden days of steam, it has one of the largest and most impressive collections of steam engines, carriages and steam memorabilia in

"Walk right alongside the tracks with the great beasts towering above"

the country. The collection is held on track and sidings alongside Didcot railway station, and is lovingly cared for by members of the Great Western Railway Society, from whose 8,000 members come volunteers who will readily strip down an engine at the drop of a spanner, or regale visitors with tales from the glory days.

The museum makes a great day out with young children. There are about 20 to 25 actual steam engines – including the beasts the King Edward II and the Caerphilly Castle, both TGV's of their day. Many are operational and can be seen in action on the steam days, whilst on other days you can still see them and climb up on them. With the driving wheels standing taller than a man, the sheer scale of these mighty engines creates an awe-inspiring sense of power, setting Didcot apart from many of the more usual steam enthusiasts' railways.

There is heaps to see and do: we walked right alongside the tracks with the great beasts towering above, enjoyed clambering up into the engine driver's compartments in the engine sheds and relaxed in 1930's carriages pulled short distances down the line by puffing, whistling steam trains. There was plenty of activity with lots of shunting backwards and forwards and engines and carriages being moved to and fro. We just missed seeing the huge turntable in operation, but were assured that it is so finely balanced that it only takes two or three men to turn an engine (as they can weigh 175 tons this seemed an incredible feat!). It is safe enough for children, but if you are nervous take reins for toddlers.

Apart from the engine sheds, the site has many other railway relics. We liked the 24-lever 1898 Radstock North signal box (winner of the 1989 Best Restored Signal Box Award – how many signal boxes are restored each year, we asked ourselves?), which you can sometimes see in operation, and the carriage shed full of restored, partly

restored and just plain salvaged carriages. The Relics Museum is an indoor collection of bits and pieces, including a re-created station master's office, railway toys and model trains (attracting several fascinated children to jostle for position on the kid's viewing platform).

There is a typical station restaurant with Formica-topped tables, smelling of chips and with the requisite steamy windows and mugs of strong tea. There is also a grassy picnic area with tables and benches, and two shops – the bookshop with a mix of Thomas The Tank toys and real train-spotters equipment, and the relics shop, selling railway magazine archive material.

Special events are held throughout the year: Santa Specials, Easter Egg hunts, and Thomas the Tank Engine days. Although not really a wet weather day out, do try a winter trip as the steam shows up better in colder weather.

Didcot will make a train-spotter of the best of you. We restrained ourselves from buying the tapes of engine steam sounds, but our daughter is still saving for the £1,500 hire fee for the 3288 freight engine – anyone got a few miles of railway track we can borrow?

Fact File

- ● ADDRESS: Didcot Railway Centre, Didcot, Oxfordshire
- ● TELEPHONE: 01235 817200
- ● WEBSITE: www.Didcotrailwaycentre.org.uk
- ● DIRECTIONS: Signposted from junction 13 of the M4
- ● PUBLIC TRANSPORT: Regular fast trains from Paddington to Didcot Parkway (about 1 hours trip)
- ● DISTANCE: 53 miles
- ● TRAVEL TIME: 1 hour 30 minutes
- ● OPENING: Static days weekends all year, daily half terms and from beginning April to end of September, 10.00am-5.00pm or dusk. Steam days on most Sundays from March and also Wednesdays during the summer
- ● PRICES: Adults £6.50, children £4.50, under-5's free, family ticket £19.00. Reduced prices on static days
- ● RESTAURANT FACILITIES: Yes
- ● NAPPY CHANGING FACILITIES: Yes
- ● HIGH CHAIRS: No
- ● DOGS: Yes
- ● PUSHCHAIR-FRIENDLY: Yes
- ● NEARBY: Childe Beale wildlife park (01734 845172)

Roald Dahl Children's Gallery

THIS IS A REALLY FUN MUSEUM PACKED WITH EXPERIMENTS, TRICKS AND games based on the crazy ideas and inventiveness of Roald Dahl, who used to live locally. Everything you and the kids love about this inspirational children's author is here – the wonder, weirdness and wackiness. Adjacent to the Buckinghamshire County Museum, it is a very small museum, with timed admittance for one hour only, so bear in mind that at peak times you will not be able to stay for a lengthy period and see the suggestions below for what else to do in the area. Be warned too, no pushchairs are allowed inside, so if this applies to you, you'll have to carry the babe, wear a baby carrier, or do what we did, which was to just let him crawl around the floor (a bit hair-raising at times).

Walking into the Gallery you pass the oh-so-wonderful Glass Elevator, which is painted with gaily coloured sweets and has a surprise in the doors.

"Inside the Gallery is a cacophony of riot and colour"

Inside the Gallery is a cacophony of riot and colour. The children were off – excitedly operating buttons and levers, whilst we adults tried to keep up whilst feverishly doing all the experiments ourselves. There are levers to pull, buttons to press, costumes to try on, experiments to spin: all highly ingenious interpretations of events and characters from Roald Dahl's stories. If you do know the stories well you can have great fun spotting familiar scenes, but if you don't, it doesn't matter, it will just make you want to read them.

Downstairs you'll find sound experiments, a Giant Peach complete with bugs and beasties and some different ways of looking at them, the Fantastic Fox tunnel (our childrens' favourite), and nasties in Miss Catchpole's cupboard (if you dare). Upstairs is devoted to light and visual effects: cameras, chromakey and a whole array of optical tricks and illusions. The kids were absorbed by the simplest things – the organ pipes and the shadow-making machine (I hope the shadow of us kissing isn't still there?), whilst I, for one, loved the little details like the replacement hip joint door handle!

Everything is very well-explained, if you can find time to read notices before the kids drag you off, and with many imaginative tricks to encourage children to get involved, such as notices written in mirror writing. The museum staff are fun and very helpful: one persisted with the cocktail stick and gramophone experiment for ages until my somewhat clumsy four-year-old managed to hear the orchestra.

For somewhere to make you think, challenge your perceptions and make finding out fun, the Gallery is one of the best. You'll find your hour passes all too quickly, but when you emerge go in to the adjoining Bucks County Museum which is new, attractive and not at all like a fusty

old museum. The displays are mostly grouped around local themes, for example brickmaking, illustrated by carefully modelled scenarios incorporating artefacts from the past, interactive areas with drawers to pull and questions to answer. There is a shop (lots of Road Dahl merchandise) and a small attractive cafe with some nice tables in the tiny garden.

Try walking up the lane to the church and into the church yard, or pick up a leaflet on the Rock Walk from the County Museum shop. This is an hour-long trail round the side streets of this pretty little market town. The Friars Shopping Centre was warm and welcoming when we went on a cold November day and there is a 10-pin bowling alley in there. Further afield you could try the Bucks Goat Centre 3 miles south of Aylesbury, open Tuesdays to Sundays 10.00am-5.00pm (01296 612983) or RHS's Waddesdon Manor Garden (01296 651142), a Victorian garden open Wednesdays to Sundays and Bank holidays 10.00am-5.00pm (closed January and February).

Fact File

- ADDRESS: Church Street, Aylesbury, Buckinghamshire
- TELEPHONE: 01296 331441
- DIRECTIONS: M25 junction 20 and A41 to Aylesbury. Park in city centre car park and walk to Museum
- PUBLIC TRANSPORT: Train from London Marylebone
- DISTANCE: 40 miles
- TRAVEL TIME: 1 hour
- OPENING: Peak times are 10.00am-5.00pm Saturdays and school holidays, 2.00pm-5.00pm Sundays, with timed tickets and restricted numbers. Booking possible (£1.00 charge). Off-peak time daily 3.00-5.00pm
- PRICES: £3.50 adults, £2.50 children, under-3's free. Reduced prices off-peak times. Includes admission to County Museum
- NAPPY CHANGING FACILITIES: Yes
- HIGH CHAIRS: Yes
- RESTAURANT FACILITIES: Yes
- DOGS: No
- PUSHCHAIR-FRIENDLY: No
- NEARBY: Bucks Goat Centre (01296 612983), Waddesdon Manor RHS garden (01296 651142)

Syon Park Butterfly House & Aquatic Centre

ON A COLD OR DULL DAY, A VISIT TO THE WARM BUTTERFLY HOUSE with its brightly-coloured tropical flowers and the steamy Aquatic centre next door, takes some beating. In the vicinity you'll also find a delightful park to wander in, the Snakes and Ladders indoor adventure area, a large garden centre, National Trust shop, art shop, wholefood shop and restaurant facilities.

Feeding time at the Aquatic Centre takes place most days between 1.00-1.30pm and is not to be missed, as long as you are not too squeamish, that is. Piranha fish will devour their unmentionable small creatures in less than 30 seconds right in front of your eyes. The crocodiles have a lazier approach to their prey, but it still disappears pretty smartly. Huge fish, snakes, spiders, millipedes, lizards and frogs stare goggle-eyed at you a few inches away

"Huge fish, snakes, spiders, millipedes, lizards and frogs stare goggle-eyed at you"

behind the glass. Eat your heart out James Henry Trotter, these underwater viewing areas offer plenty of chances for nose-to-nose contact! Although the Centre is small, for kids with a reptilian bent, it's not to be missed, and for the brave there are even daily handling opportunities with the snakes and lizards. On the day we visited we got to hold a boa constrictor – admittedly only a baby, but still as thick, and longer than, my arm.

Outside the Centre you can have a go at pond dipping with nets provided, and the chance to examine your catch under a microscope. There is also a panning for gold game too.

☞   Life's more gentle next door with the butterflies. When
you first walk in, it takes a few minutes for your eyes to
adjust to the fact that there are butterflies everywhere.
Fluttering through the air, sitting lazily stretching their
wings on paths and foliage, hidden in leaves, big ones,
small ones, still ones and active ones. You will see most
butterflies on bright and sunny days, but even on a dull
day there should be a minimum of 500 on display at any
one time, and up to 60 different species. The colours are
fantastic: vivid oranges, yellows, viridians, in a huge
variety of stripes, spots and leopard skins. And as for
size, they range from tiddlers about an inch across, to the
huge Owl butterflies (about five inches) and Giant Atlas
Moths (a stupendous seven inches).

Their greenhouse is subdivided
into several sections. There
is a small stream running
through, little bridges and
pools with terrapins and
fish to captivate children,
and exotic fragrances
meandering in the heavy
air. There are archways
laden with tropical
blossom, pergolas, and
benches where you can sit
and watch, trying to
match the
butterflies you can see
with those on the
identification charts.
Identification leaflets are on
sale in the shop for 60p each
or you can use the boards
inside the butterfly house.
The emerging cages near the
entrance give the chance to
watch butterflies coming
out from the pupae
stages, and you can
also see caterpillars on

the underside of some leaves.

Most of the butterflies are in the tropical sections. However, from May to September, British butterflies are on display in an adjoining area. At the exit is a small insect gallery: giant millipedes, lizards, tarantulas and the like. Toddlers really need to be lifted up for a good view here. There is also a very good shop, with small toys, wall charts and books, on a general nature theme.

The adjacent Syon Park Gardens are a good way to extend your day once you've finished: 55 acres of Capability Brown landscaped parkland, making a very pleasant walk at any time of year. It costs about £2.50 for adults, and £2.00 for children. There is a large lake running through the middle (beware – it is unfenced), plenty of ducks, many fine big trees, fallen trunks to clamber on and sequences of hidden ponds and waterfalls which can keep children amused for ages. It is peaceful and quiet, with all paths suitable for pushchairs. There is plenty of room to picnic.

Fact File

- ADDRESS: London Butterfly House and Aquatic Centre, Syon Park, Brentford, Middlesex
- TELEPHONE: 0208 560 7272 (Butterfly House), 0208 847 4730 (Aquatic Centre)
- WEBSITE: www.aquatic-experience.org
- DIRECTIONS: South Circular (A205) to Kew Bridge, then turn left down the A315 towards Twickenham. Signposted 'Syon House'
- PUBLIC TRANSPORT: Train from Waterloo, to Kew Bridge station, then 237 or 267 bus to Brentlea Gate (50 yards to pedestrian entrance)
- DISTANCE: 12 miles
- TRAVEL TIME: 30-45 minutes
- OPENING: Butterfly House daily 10.00am-5.30pm (summer) or 3.30pm (winter). Aquatic Centre daily 10.00am-6.00pm (summer) or 4.30pm (winter)
- PRICES: Butterfly House £3.20 adults, £1.90 children, under-3's free, family ticket £7.50. Aquatic Centre £3.50 adults, £3.00 children, under-3's free
- RESTAURANT FACILITIES: Yes
- NAPPY CHANGING FACILITIES: Yes, by shop and garden centre
- HIGH CHAIRS: Yes
- DOGS: No
- PUSHCHAIR-FRIENDLY: Yes
- NEARBY: Kew Bridge steam museum (0208 568 4757) for working steam machinery (in steam weekends only)

Woburn Safari Park

Nothing quite like it for
cooling the blood . . .

GUARANTEED TO AWE EVEN THE MOST ARDENT TIGER-SPOTTER, TRY A trip here if you *really* want to get close to the animals. Probably not a good visit on a hot day, but in cool, windy or even rainy weather, Woburn makes a great action-packed day out. Get here early as there is plenty to do.

As we drove in, the sight of a couple of elephants standing casually by the roadside instantly raised an enthusiastic response. Unlike adults, children never seem to find such sights incongruous. If you've not been to a Safari Park before, note that the idea is to drive round amongst the animals, literally. Once you have started on the circuit, chances to pull-in are limited, you cannot get out of your car, and in many places you must have all windows shut. It is essential to do a toilet, food/drink and stretch-legs stop before you start, so we duly headed for the Safari Lodge area first.

"We bumped straight into a group of tigers at feeding time"

Fully refreshed and raring to go we started out. Wow! Within minutes you see elephants, rhinos and zebras parading within yards of the car. With no fences, you get a great view. Proceeding as slowly as possible round the park, we lingered over the hippos, who looked like islands in the mud and sympathised with the giraffes, whose long necks make grass grazing an ungainly business.

More excitement was yet to come. Stern notices and heavy-duty security systems indicate that you are entering the Big Cat areas. Once through the automatic gates we bumped straight into a group of tigers at feeding time. The sight of them drooling over hunks of meat is not for the faint-hearted or vegetarian. We drove on round past leggy wolves with mean yellow eyes (Mowgli's family was mentioned by someone in the back seat) and into the lion enclosure. Here the lions loll disdainfully in the grass, and although there are rangers around in jeeps, you have a disconcerting impression that you are alone in the savannah with them.

On further, and into the monkey and bear woods. Don't go in here if you have any loose bits on your car. The monkeys were convinced we were hiding food under the bonnet, and gave us a thorough going-over. The highlight for the kids, though, was a monkey pooing on the windscreen!

The round trip takes about 45 minutes, depending on how slowly you drive. You can go round as many times as you like, so you get a chance to see a constantly changing kaleidoscope of activity, and the slow pace is good for putting fractious babies to sleep.

When you tire of driving round, head back to the Safari Lodge area. As well as offering picnic areas and restaurants, all day long there are animal encounter opportunities and demonstrations. Don't miss elephant

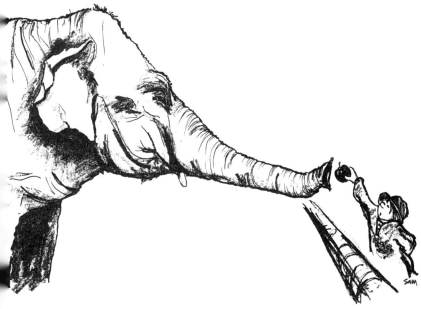

feeding when our kids got the chance to hold out apples for the huge animals to take with their prehistoric trunks. There are sealions, penguins, birds of prey, parrots doing tricks, and plenty of opportunity to let off steam with some excellent play areas. The Adventure Ark and bobcat ride are amazing for older children, whilst the Safari trail kept the younger ones busy for some time. Both these, and several of the demonstrations are under cover. Also, for a different view of the animal reserve, a small open train gives 20-minute rides through the bison park.

Finally, the entrance fee covers admission to Woburn Abbey Deer Park. This is large grassy parkland with magnificent oak trees for scrambling on. Great for running around or picnicing, it is much quieter than the Safari Park and makes a good end to the day.

Fact File

- ADDRESS: Woburn Safari Park, Woburn, Bedfordshire
- TELEPHONE: 01525 290407
- WEBSITE: www.woburnsafari.co.uk
- DIRECTIONS: On the A4012 about four miles from M1 motorway (Exit 13). Follow signs to the Safari Park
- PUBLIC TRANSPORT: None
- DISTANCE: 45 miles
- TRAVEL TIME: 1 hour 15 minutes
- OPENING: Daily from beginning of March to the end of October, 10.00am-5.00pm. Weekends only during the winter 11.00am-3.00pm
- PRICES: £12.50 adults, £9.00 children, under-3's free. Family reductions available. Reduced price outside of school holidays
- RESTAURANT FACILITIES: Yes
- NAPPY CHANGING FACILITIES: Yes
- HIGH CHAIRS: Yes
- DOGS: No, kennels provided
- PUSHCHAIR-FRIENDLY: Yes
- NEARBY: Woburn Abbey, with its deer park, antiques shops and tour of the stately home

The Great Outdoors

Audley End House & Country Park

FOR A STUNNING DAY OUT IN SPLENDID SURROUNDINGS COME TO Audley End, where you'll find a vast Jacobean mansion, extensive 'Capability Brown' parkland and a miniature railway to boot. With so much on offer, everyone in the family should be able to find something to suit them. The overwhelming impression is one of grand scale here, you almost feel as if you've been abroad after a visit without having even left this country!

"The River Cam runs along the edge of the grounds and is lovely for pottering along and playing pooh-sticks"

The main enjoyment for those with children is to be found outside in the substantial grounds. Start with the Parterre gardens in front of the house, where you can enjoy hide and seek amongst the formal hedges. I'm sure they were not designed for this, but the maze of borders in glorious colours are just the right height for toddlers to play peek-a-boo.

The rest of the gardens roll around, behind and in front of the house. You can strike out in any direction you fancy and will soon escape the madding crowds. Up to the Greek Temple is a good way to appreciate the grandeur of the house and landscaped gardens, and you can wander all over and find all sorts of treasures to explore. It can be a bit rough underfoot, but the footpaths are fine for pushchairs and there are plenty of good picnic spots to be claimed throughout the park. Children can shout, jump and generally run riot at will, and even adults can too!

Our favourite walk is to follow the footpaths down from the house towards the river. Here the River Cam runs along the edge of the grounds and although really just a big stream, it is lovely for pottering along and playing 'pooh-sticks'. It opens into a small lake which has endless duck-feeding possibilities in the shape of an array of ever-hungry and noisy ducks in all sizes, shapes and colours. Nearby is Robert Adam's neo-classical tea-house bridge, which is very attractive, surrounded by intimate gardens and little summer houses that our daughter thinks are Wendy Houses placed there purely for her benefit.

The highlight of the day for most children will probably be the steam train ride, which is to be found over the road from the house. It takes you on an enchanting short ride past wooden stations complete with sign posts and soft toy station masters. Toys gaze down at the passengers from little bridges spanning the line, and colour-co-ordinated teddies, Ruperts and Paddingtons cluster in the trees having tea, playing games and swinging in the branches. It's all about watching out for the next lot of toys and who can spot them first, with lots of questions like "Do they stay out all night?", and "Don't they get cold, Mummy?" A short tunnel with ghost noises and screams adds to the fun. When you've finished you can get drinks and ices served from a real double decker bus,

and relax in the picnic area to watch the comings and goings of the engines. The railway is an independent venture to the Audley End Estate, but you can go between the two if you keep your tickets. Trains should run at weekends from 1st April to 29th October, and daily during the school holidays in that period (check times on 01799 541354). They cost £2.00 for adults and £1.00 for children.

Don't go inside the house with young children unless you can't bear to miss the beautiful decor, sumptuous paintings and period furniture. We have just about managed it with our lot, but the atmosphere is rather one of hushed tones and reverent appreciation. Having said that, our daughter was fascinated by the enormous Victorian dolls' house with all its living rooms and dining rooms. You can't take your own pushchairs and backpacks around the house, but a lightweight buggy, baby slings, reins and wrist straps can be borrowed.

The Brewhouse and Garden exhibition is worth a visit if you can't face the grandness of the house: it shows a history of the house and estate, with the skullery and wash rooms being just some of the things to see.

Fact File

- ADDRESS: Audley End House & Park, Saffron Walden, Essex
- TELEPHONE: 01799 522399
- DIRECTIONS: M11 junctions 8 or 9 (northbound only) and B1383 towards Saffron Walden. Signposted
- PUBLIC TRANSPORT: None
- DISTANCE: 55 miles
- TRAVEL TIME: 1 hour 30 minutes
- OPENING: 11.00am-5.00pm Wednesdays to Sundays and Bank Holidays from 1 April to 29th October
- PRICES: Adults £4.50, children £2.30, family £11.30 (grounds only). House and grounds adults £6.50, children £3.30. Under-5's free
- RESTAURANT FACILITIES: Yes
- NAPPY CHANGING FACILITIES: Yes
- HIGH CHAIRS: Yes
- DOGS: No
- PUSHCHAIR-FRIENDLY: Yes
- NEARBY: Duxford Airfield (01223 835000) for a chance to look over Concorde, and any number of other civil and military aircraft

Blenheim Palace

MAKE THE TREK TO BLENHEIM PALACE WHEN EVERYONE IS IN THE mood for a real day out. Despite it being a long journey, there are several attractions there to tempt you: formal gardens and terraces, great walks in the expansive Capability Brown park and a wide lake. For children there is a Pleasure Garden, with a walled games area, butterfly house, adventure playground and mini train ride down.

Start with a brisk tour round the outside of the Palace itself. Its vast golden sandstone bulk may momentarily awe any child. Walk through the arches in the main courtyard to the patio overlooking the Italianate Sunken Garden with ponds and fountain. There are a series of grand formal terraces with statues and obelisks. Bribe the kids with an ice-cream from the cafe nearby and then head off back in front of the Palace to the more open parkland where there are less 'Keep Off' notices and flat lawns for scampering over.

Away from the Palace there are steep slopes down to the lake which the children will enjoy tumbling down. You can follow the road round the side to the bridge if you prefer, and then go on through the park on a wide open path – ideal for toddlers and pushchairs. There are lovely views and easy walks on two marked circuits: the Fisheries Cottage walk taking about half an hour (don't miss the teeming trout in the lake inlet), or a longer walk through the park which takes about an hour. Look out for sheep and lambs in the spring.

"Lovely views and easy walks on two marked circuits"

On the lake you can hire rowing boats for a small charge. The boats are not hired out in windy weather. There is a picnic area down by Queen Pool with tables and seats, and you can dip your toes in in warm weather. Swimming is not advised though!

The Pleasure Garden is a 10-minute walk from the Palace itself. If you don't fancy the walk, there is a small single gauge railway that gets there in a few minutes, running from near the car park by the Palace. Trains run from 11.00am-5.30pm, departing every half an hour. You may have to queue, particularly around lunch time. Similarly, the last trains back in the evening often fill up.

The highlights of the Pleasure Garden are within a walled games area. To enter this costs £1.50 for adults, and £1.00 for children. Pushchairs would need to be left at the entrance. Inside the walled area is a large grassy play space, bisected by several paths and with a central fenced-off pond. The Marlborough Maze lies to the left, and is great fun. We solved the maze in about 20 minutes. Admittedly, this was with a great deal of cheating on the part of certain small people, who had a tendency to wriggle through gaps in the hedges!

Our children had a lot of fun running around on the large plastic puzzle path, and hi-jacking the over-sized chess men and horses from the adjacent chess set. They also enjoyed the model village, although only one street long, it is crammed with tiny windows and courtyards for peering in. There is also a bouncy castle for two-to-five-year-olds. Outside of the walled games area the butterfly house is well worth a visit, although a bit narrow to negotiate with buggies. Also outside, the adventure playground is impressive, with a separate area for under-5's.

Eating facilities are good, with a spacious cafe in the Pleasure Gardens serving sandwiches, hot snacks, drinks and cakes. It has a terrace and lawn outside with benches and tables. However, on a sunny day you could not do better than take a picnic into the main park and admire the grandeur of the site whilst munching!

Fact File

- ADDRESS: Blenheim Palace, Woodstock, Oxfordshire
- TELEPHONE: 01993 811325 or 01993 811091 weekdays
- WEBSITE: www.blenheimpalace.com
- DIRECTIONS: M40 to junction 9, A34 towards Oxford, and follow signs
- DISTANCE: 70 miles
- TRAVEL TIME: 1 hour 45 minutes
- OPENING: Pleasure Garden and Palace from mid March to end October daily from 10.30am-4.45pm. The park is open all year 9.00am-4.45pm
- PRICES: All-inclusive ticket £8.50 adults, £4.50 children, family £22.00, under-5's free
- RESTAURANT FACILITIES: Yes
- NAPPY CHANGING FACILITIES: Yes
- HIGH CHAIRS: Yes
- DOGS: Yes
- PUSHCHAIR-FRIENDLY: Yes
- NEARBY: The Trout Inn on the Thames, on the outskirts of Oxford at Wolvercote, with an adjacent ruined nunnery making a nice picnic spot

Groombridge Place Gardens

Ahh – there be wild things . . .

IF YOU RELISH A SENSE OF MYSTERY AND INTRIGUE YOU WILL NOT BE disappointed by a visit here. At an everyday level it has walled gardens, a forest, a canal, and birds of prey demonstrations, within a wonderful period setting. It also has an uncanny feel of magic about it. The setting for a Sherlock Holmes novel and the Draughtsman's Contract, you'll feel the urge to keep your ears pricked for the tinkle of feminine laughter behind the hedge or your eyes peeled for a sudden shadow on the path.

An ideal setting for fantasy games, the walled gardens are a series of 'rooms' with interconnecting paths lined with tall hedges. See if you can work out the purpose of the fountain in the Drunken Garden or stroke the nose of one of the huge goldfish there: if you chance to trail your fingers in the water they will undoubtedly come up for a look. The mis-shapen yews, gnarled and twisted trunks of maples, and odd statues heighten the sense of unreality in the gardens. Look out for the giant in the Priest's House, the figures in the hedge and pike in the dark waters of the moat.

"It has an uncanny feel of magic about it"

See the times of the birds of prey demonstrations at the entrance – usually there are three a day – and they are not to be missed. The birds are brought out of the aviary, tethered on posts about 12' away from you, and then individually fly freely in the adjacent field. The sight of the 7' wing-spanned sea eagle soaring overhead, or the hawk skimming across the ground is enough to impress any child. We also saw several owls, a falcon, kestrel and buzzard. All are introduced to the audience by name, children can get close to them, and some even do a little walk-about amongst the audience.

You can get a canal boat ride up to the Enchanted Forest (about £1.00 per person). As it was a hot day on our visit we took the boat, a shady and gentle 10-minute ride. Our kids loved stretching out to grab passing leaves and there are kingfishers to watch out for on the way. Alternatively, you can walk along the path next to the canal or go up through the vineyard.

The aptly-named Enchanted Forest is a delight. A stream tumbles down from the silent waters of a spring-fed pool, with waterfalls and little bridges, ideal for fishing with sticks. Wellies are probably advisable, especially after wet weather. There are plenty of fairy glens, fallen branches and clinging creepers. The new Creature Park has wallabies and llamas in giant enclosures. The Dark Walk is fantastic boardwalk through the woods: suspended above the forest floor on steps, tunnels and platforms you can watch out for trolls below and play all sorts of games. Set off from the main path, pushchairs

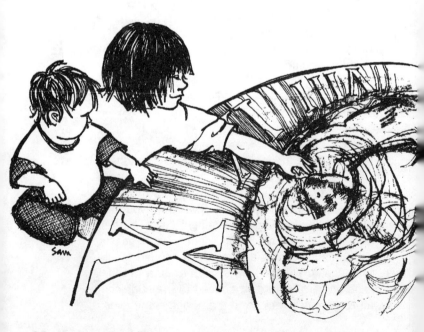

would have to give it a miss, although the rest of the paths are manageable for pushchairs. Watch out for loads of really ingenious suprises and let your imaginations run wild – the Forest is a wonderful place to let the kids have free rein. They'll rush off having their own adventures and making their own discoveries: a giant swing, trees with faces, a totem pole, a spider's lair, a wigwam. One mystery follows another to keep you all guessing and enthralled.

Back at the entrance you will find good facilities: a tea room, toilets, a creative gift shop, and a couple of pleasant picnic areas with both sunny and shaded areas. Be prepared to be watched over by peacocks as you eat.

There are lots of special events throughout the year: Robin Hood days, family fundays, scarecrow extravaganzas and craft days. For an extra treat you can even arrive at Groombridge by steam train now: Spa Valley railway trains leave from Tunbridge Wells station (Sainsbury's car park) for a 15-minute ride through beautiful countryside to Groombridge.

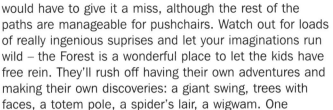

Fact File

- ADDRESS: Groombridge Place, Groombridge, Tunbridge Wells, Kent
- TELEPHONE: 01892 863999
- WEBSITE: www. groombridge.co.uk
- DIRECTIONS: On the B2110, just off the A264 between Tunbridge Wells (A21 from London) and East Grinstead (A22 from London)
- PUBLIC TRANSPORT: Tunbridge Wells station with trains from Charing Cross is a short steam train or bus ride away
- DISTANCE: 40 miles
- TRAVEL TIME: 1 hour 15 minutes
- OPENING: Daily 9.00am-6.00pm from Easter to 31 October
- PRICES: Adults £7.50, children £6.50, under-4's free, family £25.00
- RESTAURANT FACILITIES: Yes
- NAPPY CHANGING FACILITIES: Yes
- HIGH CHAIRS: Yes
- DOGS: No
- PUSHCHAIR-FRIENDLY: Yes
- NEARBY: Royal Tunbridge Wells, a haven of Georgian shops and sights. Try the 'A Day at the Wells' historical performances at the Corn Exchange (01892 546545)

Hatfield House

*I have the heart and stomach of a king
and of a king of England too . . .*

A VISIT TO HATFIELD HOUSE PROVIDES YOU WITH A GLIMPSE OF A
moment in history as well as offering a delightful haven of
peace and tranquillity just 20 miles from the hustle and
bustle of Central London. The House's chief claim to
historical fame is that it was here, sitting under an oak
tree in the gardens, that Elizabeth I heard of her
accession to the throne, and wandering through the
extensive grounds it is easy to recapture that moment.

Hatfield House however has a great many pleasures to
offer in addition to those of historical contemplation, in
particular the rolling parkland and gardens. There are a
number of marked walks around the park, one to the site
of 'Queen Elizabeth's Oak', or you can wander through
woodlands and along lake sides, taking in a wealth of
wildlife. The walks take
you well away from the
house, and with babies
you would be better off
using a backpack rather
than a pushchair because
the ground is a bit rough.
However, the main
gardens and extensive
shrubbery next to the house are all easily accessible for
buggies. The West Garden – the main formal, cultivated
gardens – is a toddler's delight as it consists of lots of
little 'rooms', some with fountains in the centre, others
with herbs, and often split by toddler-height hedges.
Water and fountains around do mean that you need to
keep an eye on the children before they decide to join
the large, fat fish in the ponds!

Alternatively, wander in the 'Wilderness Garden', a sea
of daffodils in the spring and glorious colours in the
autumn as the leaves begin to turn. This is a very

**"Wander through
woodlands and along
lake sides, taking in
a wealth of wildlife"**

peaceful, special place with lots of room for children to roam in a safe and interesting environment. The ban on dogs gives it particular appeal (to non dog-owners!). We relaxed here whilst the children searched for twigs, all of us basking in the September sun.

The House itself is open to the public with hourly guided tours every day except Sunday. Buggies are allowed around the House but there is a certain amount of carrying to be done to get upstairs. The main house was built in Jacobean times by Robert Cecil and remains

☞ the family home of the Cecils. Only one wing of the old Palace in which Henry VIII housed his children now remains, adjacent to the main house. There are tapestries, fine portraits and armour to be seen, but the model soldiers exhibition (3,000 toy soldiers in battle and display positions) is likely to be most of interest to children.

Back outside again, there is a very well laid-out playground area with picnic tables provided and lots of room, all in a pretty setting surrounded by trees and countryside. As well as swings and wooden play equipment, there is a track to test whether you can get round without touching the ground: this was our daughter's favourite attraction in the playground as she hopped from tree stump to tree stump!

For practicalities the stable area is the place to head for. There is a large, airy cafe with plenty of outdoor seating and a shop. It has lots of room for buggies (even double ones) and a reasonably varied choice of food. There is a mother and baby room in the ladies loo.

Fact File

- ADDRESS: Hatfield House, Hatfield, Hertfordshire
- TELEPHONE: 01707 262823
- DIRECTIONS: On the A1000 Great North Road, accessible from the A1(M). Signposted, and next to Hatfield train station
- PUBLIC TRANSPORT: Regular train service from Kings Cross to Hatfield
- DISTANCE: 20 miles
- TRAVEL TIME: 45 minutes
- OPENING: From 25 March to 24 September (except Good Friday). Park, nature trail and play area daily from 10.30am-8.00pm, gardens 11.00am-6.00pm. House, restaurant and shop closed Monday
- PRICES: Park £1.80 adults, 90p children, under-5's free. Gardens and house £6.20 adults, £3.10 children. Different rates for special events
- RESTAURANT FACILITIES: Yes
- NAPPY CHANGING FACILITIES: Yes
- HIGH CHAIRS: Yes
- DOGS: No
- PUSHCHAIR-FRIENDLY: Yes
- NEARBY: Mill Green Water Mill (01707 271362), a working water mill on the River Lee

Knebworth House

IF KNEBWORTH HOUSE MEANS ROCK CONCERTS AND DISTANT memories of child-free days, think again! It offers a comprehensive day out for the family, with an extensive park, gardens and a magnificent stately home, all complemented by a children's adventure area at Fort Knebworth.

The house is wonderfully impressive with Gothic battlements and grinning heraldic beasts to spot. Outside you can admire the pinnacles and statuary and explore the formal gardens arranged around the house: a delightful herb garden, rose garden, ponds and fountains are all to be investigated. A large tree with branches descending to the ground provided our daughter with at least half an hour's entertainment as she learnt the finer points of tree climbing.

Further afield, the grassy 250-acre park offers plenty of space to run about and is ideal for walks and picnics. Keep an eye out for the herds of Red and Sika deer who inhabit the park. There are gravel paths near the house and some other footpaths, so as long as it's not too wet, you'll be able to explore quite adequately with a pushchair.

> **"An impressive large house with Gothic battlements and grinning heraldic beasts to spot"**

The church is a few minutes' walk from the house and is worth a visit to see its tiny cluttered graveyard, full of jumbled history and the impressively-carved tombs inside, with their wealth of detail on the costumes and characters of a forgotten era.

Knebworth House itself is the home of the Lytton family and inside retains a real sense of being a private residence, with pictures and photographs on the walls. You can't take pushchairs round, but it is sufficiently small and compact to be able to dash around with children, peer at a few family photographs, take in a little history and marvel (or grimace) at the armoury, without hitting a child's boredom threshold. In our case, it was quite the reverse as most of the rooms are only roped off, so it was more a case of persuading a curious toddler that all those interesting looking objects really weren't a wonderful new set of toys presented just for her amusement! The attendants in the house are friendly and knowledgeable, and not fazed (or they didn't show it) by the potential disruption. For older children, there are several activity booklets available which help to increase their involvement and enjoyment.

Fort Knebworth, an enclosed children's adventure playground, is about half a mile away near the park entrance. It is clearly popular with local families and there were a couple of birthday parties going on when we were there. It is quite exposed in bad weather and the only covered picnic area is a bit like a bandstand and hence

open to the elements. However, the playground itself is extensive and offers something for most age groups.

There are also a couple of extras which make it that little bit special as a place to take the children. One is the Astroglide – a giant slide which you go down sitting on special mats with a fast lane for the real thrill seekers! The corkscrew and freefall slides are great for over-6's, whilst a bouncy castle and miniature railway keep their younger brothers and sisters busy.

Several special events are held during the year: for those with children the Sealed Knot battle re-enactions would be popular or the specialist car owners' club rallies held during the summer. You can also join hour-long garden tours at £1.00 per person.

There's a cafe in an attractive 16th century tithe barn in the stable block outbuildings. It's a bit dark inside, but has tables outside so you can sit there if you want.

Fact File

- ADDRESS: Knebworth House, Knebworth, Hertfordshire
- TELEPHONE: 01438 812661
- WEBSITE: www.knebworthhouse.com
- DIRECTIONS: A1(M) junction 6 or 7. Signposted from the motorway
- PUBLIC TRANSPORT: Train to Stevenage and then 3-mile taxi ride
- DISTANCE: 35 miles
- TRAVEL TIME: 1 hour
- OPENING: Daily 11.00am-5.30pm from 27 March to 11 April and 27 May to 5 September (closed 6 June). Weekends only the rest of April, May and September
- PRICES: Gardens, park and fort £5.00 per person, under-5's free, and family tickets £17.50. All inclusive entry £6.00 adult, £5.50 children, under-5's free
- RESTAURANT FACILITIES: Yes
- NAPPY CHANGING FACILITIES: No
- HIGH CHAIRS: Yes
- DOGS: Outside only
- PUSHCHAIR-FRIENDLY: Yes, except house
- NEARBY: Benington Lordship gardens (01438 869668), Stevenage, a small hilltop garden

Painshill Park

DESIGNED IN THE EIGHTEENTH CENTURY BY AN NON-CONFORMIST landscape gardening enthusiast – Charles Hamilton – to amuse and surprise, Painshill is a garden of different moods and constantly changing vistas. There is no period mansion to distract you, simply lovely walks to romp around and a plentiful supply of grassy banks to sit on and gaze over perfectly stunning views. Full of follies, bridges and a large curving lake, Painshill has heaps of features which make it appealing for children. It seems to be little-known, despite being only a short trip from London, and its peace and timelessness are one of its great charms for adults.

The park has an intriguing history. You can even feel slightly sorry for poor old Charles – after devoting his life to creating Painshill he had to sell it in 1773 because he ran out of money! Home to Allied soldiers during the Second World War, it fell into disuse and dereliction until 1981, when the Painshill Park Trust was formed with the aim of restoring it to its former glory.

"Full of follies, bridges and a large curving lake"

It's not hard to imagine why all the volunteers

working at Painshill are so enthusiastic and friendly when you think of the thrill it must have been to uncover Gothic follies hidden for years under a tangle of weeds, or to cut back thick brambles and trees to reveal a view of majestic proportions.

A circular route goes through the garden and takes in all the main features. It is a wide smooth path, a bit steep in places, but perfectly navigable with a pushchair. The architectural features – follies, ruins, bridges and the like are ideal for children to explore. Our favourites are the Gothic temple (a "nice little house" according to our four-year-old), the Waterwheel (channels of water perfect for poking into), the fairy-like Grotto best viewed from the other side of the lake, and the imposing Gothic Tower with its 99 steps and wonderful views over the wooded Surrey countryside (may be closed sometimes). At every turn, a different portion of the magical lake comes into view: here a shimmering reflection or a couple of gliding swans, there the water lilies twitching as the tench and pike graze below, or the water surface pubescent with frog spawn in the Spring.

To follow the route without stopping would probably take about an hour and a half. However, it would be a shame to go round without pausing, indeed the best idea is to slowly meander along, stopping to rest and play in one of the countless little spots which you'll soon claim as your own favourites.

Maps are available for 30p at the entrance, and free guided tours are available summer weekends from 2.00pm. It may be worth going round with a guide on your first visit – you will get all sorts of titbits of information, and probably nearly individual attention, but it does depend on how patient your children are. If you want to go inside the waterwheel and see all the pumps and pistons in action, you do have to go in with a guide (although you could just hang around the waterwheel until a guide comes with a party and opens up).

The Gothic Tower at the far end of the park is a good place to aim for. On hot days and some weekends, there are drinks for sale at the foot of the tower. If little legs can't make it that far head for the Turkish Tent – high up above the lake and a splendid place to survey the territory you've crossed. Make your way back to the tearoom near the start of the garden to refresh yourselves.

There is a small shop next to the entrance too, and picnics are permitted in a lovely grassy field nearby.

Fact File

- ADDRESS: Painshill Park, Portsmouth Road, Cobham, Surrey
- TELEPHONE: 01932 868113
- WEBSITE: www.brainsis.com/cobham/painshill
- DIRECTIONS: Signposted off the A3, 2 miles north of the intersection with M25 (junction 10)
- PUBLIC TRANSPORT: Bus numbers 415 or 462 from Guildford Friary bus station (01737 223000 for information)or 562 from Cobham and Epsom drop you at the entrance
- DISTANCE: 25 miles
- TRAVEL TIME: 45 minutes
- OPENING: April to October 10.30am-6.00pm (last admission 4.30pm) Tuesday-Sunday and Bank Holidays. November to March 11.00am-4.00pm (last admission 3.00pm) Tuesday-Thursday, weekends and Bank Holidays
- PRICES: Adults £3.80, children £1.50, under-5's free
- RESTAURANT FACILITIES: Yes
- NAPPY CHANGING FACILITIES: Yes
- HIGH CHAIRS: No
- DOGS: No
- PUSHCHAIR-FRIENDLY: Yes
- NEARBY: Brooklands car and aircraft museum at Weybridge (01932 857381)

Penshurst Place

LOOKING FOR A HAVEN OF TRANQUILLITY, WITH PLENTY TO OFFER children as a treat? This is your place, a small stately home, surrounded by a myriad of interconnecting gardens and orchards and set in an intimate patchwork of small fields, mature hedgerows and deciduous trees.

From the car park, follow the gravel path up towards the house, and through mellow sandstone-turreted courtyards to the gardens, which radiate out in front. With a mixture of formal gardens, shady orchards (replete with polished apples when we were there), open grassy spaces and wide flower borders, great fun can be had exploring all the different nooks and crannies. Boo! We had lots of hide and seek games behind the tall box yew hedges. Beware though, there are a few deep ponds (with goldfish lurking) – so try and keep up with your little Captain Cooks. When we went it was very peaceful everywhere, but nobody seemed to mind how much noise the children made.

The medieval splendour of the house is probably left for adults to enjoy. It costs a bit more and we didn't bother, although we did peek inside the magnificent 650-year-old Baronial Hall.

However, we'd recommend a visit to the toy museum, located in a small annexe. There is no extra charge, and it makes a fascinating diversion. Our little girl loved the old-fashioned dolls and

> **"Great fun can be had exploring all the different nooks and crannies"**

teddy bears dressed in lace finery, although with lots of 'Do Not Touch' notices, our two-year-old son was something of a liability. The highlight of the museum for both of them was the Drinking Bear – so take some 2p pieces with you. Restaurant and tea-rooms are nearby.

Don't miss the magnificent adventure playground, one of the best I've seen. It has activities for all ages of children – sandpit, slides, balancing poles and swings for the younger ones, and awe-inspiring high level runs and

☞ commando-style assault courses for older athletes. The tunnel maze mound looks like it should be for older children, but our little ones soon proved us wrong – you may find keeping all the exits covered when it is time to leave quite a challenge (unless you fancy crawling inside a muddy three foot-high tunnel on your knees). Set in a lovely sunny grassy bowl, with lots of picnic tables and benches, the playground is a great place for kids to let off steam whilst you recuperate. The adjoining barn has a picnic area upstairs, agricultural and countryside exhibits,

and a small gift and tuck shop where you can pick up colouring cards, leaflets for the nature trail and things to eat.

The nature trail is rewarding. It is a mile-long walk through woods and past fishponds. It takes between 30 minutes and an hour to complete, depending on how often you stop to admire all the fauna and flora along the way. It is manageable with pushchairs in dry weather, but too muddy after a wet spell.

If you need an incentive to visit, several special events are held in the grounds during the season. There are also falconry displays held on Sundays in July and August when you can meet and handle owls, falcons and hawks. If you like cream teas, the village of Penshurst has two tearooms, whilst there are several good pubs offering tasty brews in the area for alternative lunch stops.

Fact File

- ADDRESS: Penshurst Place, Penshurst, Tonbridge, Kent
- TELEPHONE: 01892 870307
- WEBSITE: www.penshurstplace.com
- DIRECTIONS: M25 junction 5. Then A21 south, leaving at the Tonbridge North exit. Then follow the brown signs
- PUBLIC TRANSPORT: Tonbridge train station (trains from Victoria) is six miles away, with plenty of taxis available
- DISTANCE: 45 miles
- TRAVEL TIME: One hour 15 minutes
- OPENING: 10.30am-6.00pm daily from 1 April to 31 October. Weekends from beginning of March
- PRICES: Grounds only (including toy museum) £4.50 adults, £3.50 children, under-5's free, family £13.00
- RESTAURANT FACILITIES: Yes
- NAPPY CHANGING FACILITIES: Yes
- HIGH CHAIRS: Yes
- DOGS: No
- PUSHCHAIR-FRIENDLY: Yes
- NEARBY: Tonbridge Castle (01732 770929) with its re-creation of medieval life and pleasant grounds by the river

Wisley Royal Horticultural Society Gardens

With silver bells and cockle shells and pretty maids all in a row

WISLEY GARDENS ARE A TREAT – A SHORT DRIVE DOWN THE A3, plenty of room for children to safely run about, and gorgeous gardens to admire at the same time. Although really an adult outing, children are very well accommodated for. However, be warned, if you are despairing over the state of your own tangled weed-bed, the various displays of excellence will depress you even more!

The gardens are open all year, and offer something in all seasons: a carpet of daffodils in Spring in the alpine meadow, heady roses and borders in the summer, brilliant leaves of all colours to kick through in autumn and berries and fir cones to collect in the Pinetum on a bright winter's day.

"Heaps of wonderful lawns for running or crawling on"

Although not really a wet-weather day out, you can always duck into the greenhouses, with hot, warm and cool plant displays. There are heaps of wonderful lawns for running or crawling on, wide paths ideal for pushchairs (follow the wheelchair route to avoid any steps at all), and plenty of toddler-height walls for balancing practice. The gardens are large enough to get well away from everyone else if you want, and are organised into over 20 different areas, so if you go there a lot you will soon latch on to your own favourite places.

Our favourites are the Rock Garden with its myriad of little paths, streams and steps; the fruit fields and gardens, displaying a huge variety of tree and soft fruits in all sorts of forms, from those suited to small gardens to awe-inspiring fan-trained trees; and the colourful trees and heather gardens in the Pinetum and Howard's Field. Keep your eyes open for creatures as well as plants: we spotted a small snake basking in the Rock Garden one time, there are ducks and ducklings a-dabbling in the pond by the restaurant and huge goldfish will rear up from the murky depths of that same pond to snatch your bread from the surface.

There are often special family events and activities here, particularly in the summer, when you'll find extra exhibitions, workshops, competitions and displays designed to appeal to children. Throughout the year too, children can pick up and follow one of the nature trail quiz leaflets which are great fun and encourage a different view of the garden.

Other facilities at Wisley are very good. There is a large cafe, with ample space, plenty of high chairs (though none with straps), and a terrace with tables overlooking a large lawned area –

☞ ideal in the summer. Hot and cold food, drinks, cakes and snacks are available in the cafe, and there is also a more formal restaurant next door. You can't picnic in the gardens, but there is a picnic area outside, near to the car park and Wisley-grown fruit in season is sold here too from 1.15pm-4.00pm every day.

The shop next to the entrance is large and sells a variety of gifts, books and stationery. There is also a very good plant shop for shrubs, trees, bedding plants, seeds – take notes as you go around the gardens, and you can buy all the plants in the shop (you'd better leave your credit cards at home).

Fact File

- ADDRESS: Royal Horticultural Society Gardens, Wisley, Woking, Surrey
- TELEPHONE: 01483 224234
- WEBSITE: www.rhs.org.uk
- DIRECTIONS: Take A3 from London, or M25 (exit 10), follow the signs just beyond the A3 and M25 intersection
- PUBLIC TRANSPORT: Train from Waterloo or Clapham Junction to West Byfleet or Woking, and then a two-or three-mile taxi ride. Alternatively London Country Bus number 415 from Victoria
- DISTANCE: 20 miles
- TRAVEL TIME: 30 minutes
- OPENING: Monday to Saturday throughout the year. 10.00am-6.00pm in summer, 10.00am-dusk in winter. Open only to RHS members on Sundays
- PRICES: Adults £5.00, children £2.00, under-6's free. Free to RHS members
- RESTAURANT FACILITIES: Yes
- NAPPY CHANGING FACILITIES: Yes
- HIGH CHAIRS: Yes
- DOGS: No
- PUSHCHAIR-FRIENDLY: Yes
- NEARBY: The Angel Pub at Pyrford Lock on the River Wey offers pub food and welcomes families

Somewhat Historical

Amberley Industrial Museum

You won't often get the chance to ride on the top deck of a 1920's open top bus, so Amberley is almost worth a trip just for that. However, with over 20 further displays and working exhibits, there is plenty more to do, so plan to set off early and have a really full day here.

The museum consists of a series of traditional trade and crafts workshops, dotted about a 36-acre site in a reclaimed chalk pit in the beautiful South Downs countryside. On any one day you'll find many of the workshops busy with craftspeople working with traditional tools. Everyone is helpful and enthusiastic – see if you can resist your children's demands for a clay bubble pipe once they've seen the compelling demonstration! You'll come across a blacksmith, a boat builder, a besom broom maker and a potter's workshop, to name just a few. Whilst young children may not appreciate the niceties of the re-created world, they will love the bustle and older children will enjoy finding craftsmen at work; chiselling, sanding, scraping and honing.

> **"You'll come across a blacksmith, a boat builder, a besom broom maker and a potter"**

In other workshops all the tools and equipment that would have been used is laid out. The displays exhibit a meticulous attention to detail, and are fascinating for adults. It is a bit like stepping into a Sunday afternoon

☞ black and white film. There are also a couple of larger exhibition halls – notably the roadmaking museum which has some huge road building machines on display.

It's the bus and train rides that really make Amberley special for young children. The bus is wonderful. It leaves from outside the tearooms every half an hour for a 10-minute ride around the whole museum. Stopping at a number of key points, it gives a you a chance to get your bearings whilst feeling the wind in your hair and the sun on your face. A conductor comes around to collect 'fares' (you can give a donation) and hands out old-fashioned bus tickets.

Meanwhile the workman's train is on a narrow gauge railway, and gives a short steam ride through the woods in an open trailer (enclosed carriages also available). At the end of the line there is a railway museum, which includes a higgledy-piggledy assortment of steam engines and bits and pieces, ideal for scrambling all over if you are a kid! Our children also enjoyed the water pump display: plenty of opportunities to get your feet splashed here, and the electricity museum, which had buttons to press and levers to pull.

From the far end of the railway line it is about a 30-minute walk back to the tearoom and entrance, a pleasant stroll which takes you past most of the exhibits. There is also a nature trail which runs above, through the woods and offers a chance to admire the numerous wild flowers and wildlife that have colonised the chalk pits since their closure in the 1960's. The trail is not accessible with a pushchair, but the rest of the museum is.

There are special events most weekends offering extra attractions – vintage car rallies, a fire engine day, steam traction engines, and a kids' craft workshop in October. There are also Santa Special Sundays during December.

The tearoom serves hot drinks, sandwiches and limited hot meals. As an alternative you could try the Bridge Inn pub just down the road from the museum, which has a garden. You can picnic in lots of spots inside the museum, but why not walk along the banks of the nearby River Arun and spread yourselves out by the water?

Fact File

● ADDRESS: Amberley Museum, Houghton Bridge, Amberley, West Sussex
● TELEPHONE: 01798 831370
● WEBSITE: www.fastnet.co.uk/amberley.museum
● DIRECTIONS: Between Storrington and Arundel on the B2139. Follow the brown Industrial Museum signs from either the A24 or the A29
● PUBLIC TRANSPORT: Trains every hour from Victoria to Amberley . The museum is directly opposite the station
● DISTANCE: 55 miles
● TRAVEL TIME: 1 hour 30 minutes
● OPENING: From 15 March to 29 October, Wednesday to Sunday (and Bank Holiday Mondays) 10.00am-5.00pm. Daily during school holidays
● PRICES: Adults £6.25, children £3.25, under-5's free, family ticket £17.00
● RESTAURANT FACILITIES: Yes
● NAPPY CHANGING FACILITIES: Yes
● HIGH CHAIRS: No
● DOGS: Yes
● PUSHCHAIR-FRIENDLY: Yes
● NEARBY: Arundel Castle (01903 883136). River boats run to Amberley from Arundel and Littlehampton in July and August (01243 265792)

Bodiam Castle

This castle hath a pleasant seat . . .

FOR THE VERY IMAGE OF A FAIRY TALE CASTLE, COME TO BODIAM. IT IS everything children imagine a castle to be, whilst adults visiting on a quiet day, maybe at dusk as rainclouds gather, may feel a tingle in the spine picturing Macbeth and his wife plotting the demise of Duncan . . .

Bodiam is a small moated medieval castle, little more than an arrow's flight from Hastings. It has the classic square shape with round towers at each corner, beloved of children's drawings. Many of its walls, battlements and stairways are intact, making it a fine place for children to explore.

Approaching the castle on a wooden bridge over the wide moat, enormous goldfish and greedy ducks will welcome you as opposed to archers and burning oil. Once you've walked under the portcullis and through the gatehouse you are inside a grassy courtyard surrounded on all sides by the thick external walls. Low remains of internal walls are dotted around – beckoning scrambling up and jumping off, whilst the towers with their wide windowsills and keyhole-shaped slit windows overlooking the moat offer plenty of scope for peering out at imaginary raiders.

> **"A small moated medieval castle, little more than an arrow's flight from Hastings"**

Do brave the climb up the narrow spiral staircases to the upper floors. On each of the four levels in the south-east tower you'll discover a circular room with a fireplace and narrow windows, plus medieval toilets which empty straight down into the moat below! There are great views of the surrounding countryside from the top, although those with no head for heights might find the 'machicolations' a bit perturbing! (holes with sheer drops down into the moat). We enjoyed counting the stairs – "thirteen, fourteen, sixteen, four, eighteen, five, six" (there were actually 59!) – but they are very steep and uneven so be prepared for a fair amount of carrying and supervision. Pushchairs can get around most of the castle with some ingenuity, but not the upper levels.

Our children had a whale of a time shinning out of the tiny windows which are just below the level of the courtyard. They also greatly enjoyed throwing money into the spectacular well at the base of the south-east tower. Make sure you have some small change. Most areas are safely fenced where necessary, but you do need to keep an eye on very young children.

The most impressive feature of the castle is its state of preservation. You can really get a feel of what it would have been like to live here all those years ago.

Watch the short, well-produced video on the way round showing life in a medieval castle.

Off-season days you'll be likely to have the castle almost to yourself, however in the summer it is much busier. Then it is a wonderful place for picnics, though, on the grassy slopes below the castle. There is a pleasant restaurant next to the car park, which has a south facing terrace with tables overlooking the River Rother. There is also a shop selling National Trust gifts and a small museum by the castle entrance, complete with a model of the castle. For a full hands-on experience visit the new Education Base, where you can try on armour and costumes, but ring in advance to check availability as it caters for schools first.

You don't have to go into the castle, so if you'd prefer just to look at it from afar you can (you'll have to pay the car parking fee of £1.50). Spread out your meal under the noble oaks overlooking the jousting field – now occupied by sheep rather than gallant knights – or stroll along the bridleway which runs alongside.

During the summer, you can take a river boat trip from Bodiam down to Northiam and back (01797 280363). It's a pleasant excursion there on an open Sussex-built boat, and you'll pass plenty of wildlife and wild flowers during the ride: kingfishers, herons, mink and young waterfowl, to name a few. The 90-minute return trip costs £6.50 adults, £3.50 children, and the trips run at weekends from Easter, daily in the school summer holidays. Make a day of it!

Fact File

● ADDRESS: Bodiam Castle, near Robertsbridge, East Sussex
● TELEPHONE: 01580 830436
● WEBSITE: www.nationaltrust.org.uk
● DIRECTIONS: Take the A21 towards Hastings from junction 5 of the M25. Turn off at Flimwell towards Hawkshurst, and the castle is signposted from Hawkshurst
● PUBLIC TRANSPORT: None
● DISTANCE: 55 miles
● TRAVEL TIME: One hour 30 minutes
● OPENING: Daily 10.00am–5.00pm 19 February to end October. Weekends only the rest of the year
● PRICES: £3.60 adults, £1.80 children, under-5's free, family ticket £9.00. Parking £1.50
● RESTAURANT FACILITIES: Yes
● NAPPY CHANGING FACILITIES: Yes
● HIGH CHAIRS: Yes
● DOGS: No
● PUSHCHAIR-FRIENDLY: Yes
● NEARBY: Quarry Farm (01580 830670) adjacent to Bodiam

Chatham World Naval Base

Ahoy there shipmates!

THE ROYAL DOCKYARD IN CHATHAM OFFERS HOURS OF OPEN-mouthed fascination – wooden boats, lifeboats, even a real submarine – presented with imagination and flair. It's a big site though, so come early and cherry-pick.

Get a plan at the entrance: the main attractions are sprawled out in a muddle of working, restored, half-restored and just plain derelict buildings. It means there is plenty of space to run about and it all adds to the fun and sense of the sheer scale and activity of a real port. Do remember, though, it is still a working port with some cars and moving machinery around so keep your wits about you.

There is a small museum at the entrance which we went through with cries of "Look a pirate ship" (any ship with rigging and sails) and "Flag, flag" ringing out. There are lots of facts and bits of information for adults here as well as photos, exhibits and models to keep kids rushing on in excitement.

> **"We ducked through the low doors into the cramped cabin to sit in the captain's seat"**

Our first port of call was Wooden Walls, a series of interlinking tableaux recreating the construction of the Valiant, a real 18th century man'o'war, built and launched at Chatham all those years ago. Set out in the old mast house of the dockyard, it is full of massive old timbers, ships' ribs and the odd mast or two. It vividly brings the whole process of ship-building to life, can you imagine how many trees it took to build just one ship? Full of the creaks and groans of timber and rope, it is suitably gloomy and atmospheric. The timed audio-visual commentary is a bit disconcerting at first: in several places figures talk or come to life. We found it compelling, though, with lots of little details that the children could latch onto, such as the rats in the layout gallery, the anchor being forged and the cannons sticking out of the ship's side.

Outside again and on to the lifeboats – the children's favourite part of the Museum. Fancy saving lives at sea! There are dozens of lifeboats here, with ramps and walkways allowing you to walk (or run) around, above and amongst them all. Some you can go inside, and we ducked through the low doors into the cramped cabin to sit in the captain's seat and pilot the boat through the mountainous seas crashing down. Go on to play with the model boats in water tanks at the back of the hall, where you can capsize as many as you want. All around are videos and displays of life-boaters at work.

Stretch your legs and walk to the other end of the complex to the rope museum: it may well be the longest building you have ever been in. Full lengths of ropes are laid-out here, some as long as a quarter of a mile and 24" thick . You can see demonstrations of ropes being made – very noisily – with all jolly complicated twisting and pulling. Try to get an explanation of what's going on before the machines start up.

There are loads of other bits and pieces to look at in various galleries and buildings all over the site: a real ship being worked on in one dry dock, HMS Cavalier, a World War II destroyer which you can walk on above deck; a police museum complete with truncheons and old hats; and even a lovely walled garden behind the Commissioner's House. Your main problem will be fitting it all in.

Have a break in the small play area in the middle of the dockyards. It has a ship to clamber over and it made a popular R&R period with our crew. Nearby is a cafe, toilets, picnic tables and large grassy area ideal for running around. Paddle-steamer rides leave from the pier here (extra charge), or instead you can just peer over the walls at the water lurking muddily below.

Don't miss the submarine. The Ocelot is moored on the dry dock and has guided tours leaving half-hourly. The tour is a wonderful experience for any sailor-struck child. It is smelly, cramped and full of portholes and hatches to crawl through, low ceilings and steep ladders. Don't attempt it if you are claustrophobic or with a pushchair or baby backpack. That said our five-year-old loved it: laying in the bunks, the opportunity to touch and feel all sorts of switches and levers, to look through the periscope and to see the 'bombs'. "Aye, aye Cap'n!"

Fact File

- ADDRESS: Chatham World Naval Base, Kent
- TELEPHONE: 01634 823800
- WEBSITE: www.worldnavalbase.org.uk
- DIRECTIONS: M25 junction 3, or M20 junction 6. Go into Chatham and follow signs
- PUBLIC TRANSPORT: Train from Victoria or Charing Cross to Chatham. One-mile bus, taxi or walk to Dockyard from station
- DISTANCE: 40 miles
- TRAVEL TIME: 1 hour 30 minutes
- OPENING: Daily 27 March to 29 October 10.00am-4.00pm. Wednesdays and weekends in November, February and rest of March
- PRICES: Adults £8.50, children £5.50, under-5's free, family £22.50
- RESTAURANT FACILITIES: Yes
- NAPPY CHANGING FACILITIES: Yes
- HIGH CHAIRS: Yes
- DOGS: Yes
- PUSHCHAIR-FRIENDLY: Yes
- NEARBY: Fort Luton (01634 813969) models, toy museum and small animal farm

The Chiltern Open Air Museum

THIS IS A FASCINATING PLACE, OUT IN THE OPEN AIR AND WITH plenty going on to keep you interested. If it's rainy, there is always somewhere under shelter to drop into if the rain gets too much. The Museum is a collection of about 25 buildings from around Buckinghamshire that have been saved from demolition. They give a real insight into the lives and work of a rural community in the past, and particularly appealing is the collection's variety and quirkiness. There is a small playground for children but the main attraction for toddlers is exploring the buildings, whilst for older children it is to follow the nature trail and make use of the educational material. You are bound to all learn something new.

One of the first buildings you see is the Edwardian loo (or to give it its proper name – the Caversham Public Convenience), winner of a 'loo of the year' award! Further on you will find a whole range of different farm buildings including a complete Victorian farmyard, barns, a granary, a shepherd's van and a forge. More

"You'll find workers and craftsmen in period costumes, carrying out tasks in the traditional way"

unusually you can visit a 1940's prefab to provide a glimpse of more recent history and an Iron Age house to take you right back to grass roots.

There are plenty of opportunities for the children to enjoy themselves too, including a nature trail (carpeted with bluebells in spring), and farm animals as well as the buildings themselves to run riot in and explore. Our daughter's favourite experience here (apart from the Eccles cake in the cafe) was chasing after the sheep, although I'm not sure how much fun the sheep thought it was. The numerous ducks, hens, cattle (plus new-born calf when we were there) and carthorses in the farm area

really make the site live and breathe.

We especially liked the all-day-long interpretation events. Demonstrations and activities go on throughout the day, such as wash-day 1940's style, brick-making, basket-weaving and Victorian dressing-up. At weekends you'll find workers and craftsmen in period costumes, carrying out tasks in the traditional way; for example, a blacksmith, a spinner and farm workers.

The cafe is a relatively basic affair offering a small selection of snacks and cakes with some occasional hot dishes such as soup. What the facilities lack in sophistication is more than compensated for by the goodwill and enthusiasm of the staff. Pushchairs can be taken everywhere, including the nature trail. You can picnic anywhere and even the car park outside is pleasant. It opens an hour before the museum, so you can picnic there before you go in.

Fact File

● ADDRESS: The Chiltern Open Air Museum, Newland Park, Gorelands Lane, Chalfont St Giles, Buckinghamshire
● TELEPHONE: 01494 871117
● WEBSITE: www.coam.org.uk
● DIRECTIONS: M40 junction 1, take the A413 towards Chalfonts and follow the brown museum signs. From M25 junction 17, take the A405 and A412 and follow the brown cart signs
● PUBLIC TRANSPORT: Chalfont & Latimer train and tube station, then taxi
● DISTANCE: 25 miles
● TRAVEL TIME: 45 minutes
● OPENING: 1 April to 29 October, 10.00am-5.00pm daily
● PRICES: Adult £5.50, children £3.00, under-5's free, family £15.00
● RESTAURANT FACILITIES: Yes
● NAPPY CHANGING FACILITIES: Yes
● HIGH CHAIRS: No
● DOGS: Yes
● PUSHCHAIR-FRIENDLY: Yes
● NEARBY: Chalfont Shire Horse Centre (01494 872304), or Westcroft Stables Home of Rest for Horses (01494 488464) at Speen, near Great Missenden

Cutty Sark & Maritime Museum

All hands on deck!!

Shiver me timbers, landlubbers! Standing on the wooden decks of the Cutty Sark at Greenwich, and imagining the freezing waves crashing over them at 45° is enough to make you feel sea-sick, let alone thinking about climbing aloft to wrestle with salt-encrusted ropes and sails! But that was life aboard this famous sailing ship, now dry-docked in Greenwich Harbour and, together with the many other local attractions, it makes for a splendid day out.

Greenwich is easy and quick to get to, both in the car and by public transport. If you do come by car, be warned that parking can be difficult; try around the Maritime Museum or Cutty Sark jetty. Also, Greenwich is popular with tourists and often busy. It is best to get there in the morning, see the Cutty Sark and wander round the streets first, before escaping to the quieter Maritime Museum and Greenwich Park for lunch and the afternoon.

"The ship is filled plumb to the gun'ls with exciting things for kids"

The Cutty Sark is the only surviving tea clipper (a sailing boat to you and me), and was launched in 1869 for the tea trade, and later used on the wool route to Australia. When built, she was faster than steam ships, and you'll find lots of friendly guides on board who will willingly tell you (as well as many other things) that this is due to her sails, which were equal in area to 11 tennis courts (a rather bizarre unit of measurement?). Now, with her towering main mast and complex rigging, she is a

majestic sight, with wide decks which our children found to be great for tearing about on. They were also thrilled by the steep ladder stairs and awkward little doorways. The ship's Golden Rule of "one hand for the ship and one hand for yourself" is worth remembering! However, the ship is no good for pushchairs, so take backpacks for very young children.

The ship is filled plumb to the gun'ls with exciting things for kids – highlights for ours were the lurid figurehead collection in the lower hold, the Captain's cabin, the rope-handled buckets on deck, the massive wheel (actually used to steer around Cape Horn) and the crew quarters where they tried out the bunks for size (don't disturb the snoring sailor in here). Most weekends, there are lots of activities which make it special for kids, such as a real Old Salt telling sailors' yarns on the upper decks, and knot-tying demonstrations in the lower hold. On some Sundays, you may catch a troupe of shanty-singers whose lively songs make a great atmosphere.

The nearby Maritime Museum has lovely grounds you can walk around for free, with massive 32-pounder guns (great to climb on) and a playground with a wooden barge to clamber over.

Inside the Museum are galleries with model ships, sea power exhibits, costumes, the Nelson area, and new galleries emphasising the economic role of the sea. The children's hands-on gallery is called "The Bridge" and is highly interactive. Most activities are for older children (over-5's) and it can get busy at peak times, so they will have to be prepared to wait to have a go.

Greenwich, of course, has lots of other things to do. The craft market on Saturdays and Sundays has a myriad of brightly coloured stalls selling clothes, wooden toys and all sort of other craftware. It can be crowded. The extensive Greenwich Park is very hilly: great for running up hill and down dale or playing games around the trees. It has fantastic views of the Millennium Dome.

There is a cafe in the park and plenty of other choices for eating. The Pier cafe, on the harbour, is cheap for drinks and snacks and you can watch the boats going up and down the Thames.

Fact File

- ADDRESS: Cutty Sark, King William Walk, Greenwich, London
- TELEPHONE: 0208 858 3445 (Cutty Sark) and 0208 312 6602 (Maritime Museum)
- WEBSITE: www.cuttysark.org.uk
- DIRECTIONS: South Circular, A202, and signs to Greenwich on the A206
- PUBLIC TRANSPORT: Frequent trains from Charing Cross, Waterloo East, Cannon Street and London Bridge. Boats from Westminster and Charing Cross (0207 930 4097)
- DISTANCE: 15 miles
- TRAVEL TIME: 45 minutes
- OPENING: Cutty Sark 10.00am-5.00pm daily. Museum 10.00am-5.00pm daily
- PRICES: Cutty Sark adults £3.50, children £2.50, under-5's free, family £8.50. Museum adults £7.50, children free
- RESTAURANT FACILITIES: Yes
- NAPPY CHANGING FACILITIES: No
- HIGH CHAIRS: No
- DOGS: No
- PUSHCHAIR-FRIENDLY: Museum only
- NEARBY: Walk along the river to the Thames barrier

Hever Castle

*Alas, my love you have
done me wrong . . .*

MUSE ON THE TRAGEDY OF ANNE BOLEYN AS YOU STROLL AND
picnic in the grounds of her family home, where she was
courted by Henry VIII all those years ago. A Tudor
mansion rather than a castle, Hever has wonderful
gardens to play Kings and Queens in, with a water maze,
lake and Italian statues. Take towels and a change of
clothes or swimsuits on a sunny day, as you will get wet
in the water maze.

Perfect for picnics, the gardens roll down from the car
park towards the house. There are plenty of sunny banks
and mounds to spread out on, shady glens to explore,
and ornate topiary to
wonder over. Next to the
moat alongside the
house is a conventional
maze, with eight foot-
high clipped yew hedges
making cheating
impossible (we did try),
and lots of delightedly confused children.

> **"Fluttering standards, galloping hoof beats and the mock groans of the defeated"**

Further on you will find the formal gardens which have
a large number of small steps, walls and nooks and
crannies to amuse children, whilst you admire the statues
and climbing plants. Alongside, from April to October,
there is a water maze to dabble in – watch out for the
water spray when you take a wrong turn! Children really
love it, and with a sunny bank alongside to spread
yourself it is almost as much fun watching as having a
go.

For a bit of peace and quiet go beyond the formal
gardens and water maze, where you'll find the grounds
open up and run alongside a large (unfenced) lake. This
is wide and serene with low flat banks making it ideal for
poking sticks into or tossing in fir cones. The grounds are

expansive and easily swallow crowds, even on a busy summer weekend.

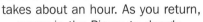

To walk all the way to the end of the lake and back takes about an hour. As you return, pause in the Piazza to dangle your feet in the fountains and admire the view over the lake. Then make your way back to the house via the formal gardens

The house is well worth a visit, although you cannot take buggies in

and with several roped-off areas be prepared to keep toddlers under control. There are many splendid tapestries and carvings, some tiny staircases and corridors to squeeze through, and a fine Tudor Long Gallery at the top of the house. The children loved the costumed figures here portraying Henry and his wives, and Anne Boleyn's life, although fortunately the details of her and her supposed lovers' fate escaped them.

Most summer weekends there are jousting displays held. You'll be invited to follow a knight on horseback, a king, queen and sundry other characters dressed up in period costumes through the grounds to the jousting field, where with much ribaldry and good-humour, a traditional tournament is re-enacted. There is lots of audience participation, with a children's parade at the beginning and everyone cheering for their own knight. With fluttering standards, galloping hoof beats and the mock groans of the defeated, it makes a vivid and exciting display. Wonderful!

Fact File

- ADDRESS: Hever Castle, Hever, near Edenbridge, Kent
- TELEPHONE: 01732 865224
- WEBSITE: www.hevercastle.co.uk
- DIRECTIONS: Take A22 south off M25 junction 6 and follow brown signs
- PUBLIC TRANSPORT: Train to Edenbridge (3-mile taxi ride) or Hever (1-mile walk) from London Victoria
- DISTANCE: 30 miles
- TRAVEL TIME: 1 hour 15 minutes
- OPENING: 11.00am-6.00pm daily 1 March to 30 November. Last admission 1 hour earlier
- PRICES: Castle and grounds £7.80 adults, £4.20 children, £19.80 family. Grounds only £6.10 adults, £4.00 children, £16.20 family. Under-5's free
- RESTAURANT FACILITIES: Yes
- NAPPY CHANGING FACILITIES: Yes
- HIGH CHAIRS: Yes
- DOGS: Yes
- PUSHCHAIR-FRIENDLY: Yes
- NEARBY: Penshurst vineyard

Mountfichet Castle & Toy Museum

Rich man, poor man,
beggar man, thief

TO GET TO GRIPS WITH THE LIFE OF THE COMMON PEOPLE 800 YEARS ago, Mountfichet is definitely the place: a re-constructed Norman motte and bailey castle and village complete with all the artefacts and true-to-life sights of the time. Children love anything grimy, and Mountfichet gives a real taste of how raw and brutish life was in those days: you won't come home dreaming of knights and courtly romance, but rather thanking your lucky stars you were born in the 20th century!

It is a compact, grassy site, surrounded by woodland and with the village and castle fenced in by Norman-style wooden fences. Inside a number of buildings are dotted about, reflecting those you would have found at the time of Norman the Conqueror: a charcoal burner's hut, pottery kiln, blacksmith, dovecotes and catapult for example. You can

> **"Peer into the dark insides of most of the buildings and rejoice in the fact you didn't have to live there"**

peer into the dark insides of most of the buildings and rejoice in the fact you didn't have to live there. All the discomfort of life is portrayed; gloomy living quarters, smoky coal fires and all the work, work, work.

Goats and sheep wander about and costumed characters such as a baron, his lady, and several peasants help give a feel to the place. You can try the village stocks for size or wonder how they ever managed to use the giant catapult. It's very interactive with lots of buttons to push, and no one says 'Don't do that' or 'Don't go in there'.

Inside the inner bailey on a small hill – the original motte – you can see the Grand Hall with a banquet laid, and the remains of the original 12th century castle. Look out for the surprise in the new look out tower and climb up the siege tower – it's only about 20' high – and wave down at anyone below. If your children are doing castles in history they will love seeing it all for 'real'.

Adjacent to the Norman village is the House on the Hill Toy Museum which, being indoors, is a good place to duck into in poor weather. It is a vast collection of teddies, dolls, toy aeroplanes, trains and dolls' houses, arranged on two floors. Plus the largest display of Action Man toys anywhere in the world! Toys from Victorian times to more recent history are here, and you'll probably recognise a good few from your own childhood. Kept in cabinets mainly, the glass reaches down to floor level in many cases so that children can get a look. Some of the toys are animated and interactive. Next door is the Rock and Roll, Film and Theatre Museum too, where you'll find many vintage slot machines.

If you come here with a picnic there's a large picnic area with tables, but expect to be joined by a number of cocks and hens. The cafe sells a limited range of refreshments. There is a souvenir shop too on the site.

A better option is to wander into Stansted, which is a very pretty old Essex village. The tea shop there serves a whole range of hot and cold food and has both indoor and outdoor seating.

The nearby Hatfield Forest is an extensive area of National Trust forest, popular with local people. It makes a great place for picnics and outdoor games, with two lakes in the centre and good family facilities.

Fact File

- ● ADDRESS: Mountfichet Castle and Museum, Stansted, Essex
- ● TELEPHONE: 01279 813237
- ● DIRECTIONS: M11 junction 8, signposted to village
- ● PUBLIC TRANSPORT: Train from Liverpool Street to Stansted Mountfichet. 3-minute walk from station
- ● DISTANCE: 35 miles
- ● TRAVEL TIME: 1 hour 15 minutes
- ● OPENING: Daily 10.00am-5.00pm, 12 March to 12 November. Toy Museum open all year
- ● PRICES: Adults £4.50, children £3.50. Toy Museum £3.50 adults, £2.50 children
- ● RESTAURANT FACILITIES: Limited
- ● NAPPY CHANGING FACILITIES: No
- ● HIGH CHAIRS: No
- ● DOGS: No
- ● PUSHCHAIR-FRIENDLY: Yes
- ● NEARBY: Stansted Airport

Museum of Kent Life

PLAY AT BEING A HOP PICKER IN THIS FASCINATING RURAL MUSEUM consisting of restored buildings, exhibitions and displays re-creating and glorifying country life in times past, here in the Garden of England. Set in 26 glorious acres of land overlooking the River Medway and running alongside Allington Lock, the location is a real treat. The whole place has a quiet, rural feel and tranquil atmosphere, especially mid-week.

Most of the buildings are down near the entrance, whilst the crops and fields that make up the rest of the museum spread up the hillside. Our children's favourites are the re-constructed hop-pickers' huts where adults can wonder at the primitive conditions endured by the annual influx of hop-pickers from London, whilst children play house in their shacks. Then there is a farm cottage to poke around, a farmhouse and an 18th century thatched barn crammed with farm implements, machinery and tractors. The 'Darling Buds of May' exhibition has lorries and a tractor, as well as re-creations of the Larkin family rooms; a bit over the heads of most young children, but ours enjoyed clambering on the truck. There are plenty of animals

"Seasonal farming activities are always on show – the grand finale being the hop-picking"

to admire in the farmyard; Rosie the Shire horse, donkeys, lambs, goats, rabbits and guinea pigs, whilst the vermin exhibition in the granary with its stuffed rats and soundtrack will give kids a thrill.

Once you've seen the buildings, walk back down towards the river past the kitchen garden, grunting pigs in the field, hops strung up high like washing on a line and the trees of traditional Kentish cobnuts. Follow the lane at the end of the car park through woods and round the back of the craft village, then up some steep steps and back across fields to the top of the museum again. It's a nice walk and takes about 30 minutes. On the way, you'll pass the M20 motorway and can marvel at the juxtaposition of the old and new.

☞ Have a quick look at the gaily painted wagons in the wagon store before rewarding yourself in the delightful tearooms, offering food and drinks, which you can eat inside or take out into the gardens

Traditional crafts such as carpentry, quilting, blacksmithing, stained glass making and potting are regularly demonstrated in the craft village, whilst seasonal farming activities are always on show – the grand finale being the hop-picking which takes place over the Harvest Weekend in September. Then, visitors can arrange to participate in the picking, if the fancy really takes them! .

Give yourself time to stroll along the riverside too, where boats are moored and ducks paddle leisurely. You can walk over the lock gates, maybe seeing them in operation, and admire the engineering of the huge sluice gates taming the flow of the river.

Fact File

- ADDRESS: Museum of Kent Life, Lock Lane, Sandling, Maidstone, Kent
- TELEPHONE: 01622 763936
- WEBSITE: www.museum-kentlife.co.uk
- DIRECTIONS: Signposted off the M20 motorway (junction 6)
- PUBLIC TRANSPORT: Train to Maidstone from Victoria, regular buses from Maidstone East to the Museum, or taxi from the station (about 2 or 3 miles)
- DISTANCE: 40 miles
- TRAVEL TIME: 1 hour 30 minutes
- OPENING: Daily 10.00am-5.30pm from 19 February to 4 November
- PRICES: Adults £4.50, children £3.00, under-5's free, family £13.00
- RESTAURANT FACILITIES: Yes
- NAPPY CHANGING FACILITIES: Yes
- HIGH CHAIRS: Yes
- DOGS: Yes
- PUSHCHAIR-FRIENDLY: Yes
- NEARBY: Rochester Castle and historic high street

Weald & Downland Open Air Museum

RURAL ARCHITECTURE MAY NOT SOUND LIKE THE MOST THRILLING WAY to amuse children, but, falling into the category of 'fascinating for adults plus safe, letting-off steam potential for children' this award-winning museum really makes a great day out. For slightly older children there is a very well-written and fun activity book to help them get the most out a visit.

This museum is unlike any other museum you may have visited. For a start it is in the open air – 55 acres of gorgeous countryside to be precise – and you are free to wander, explore and play hide and seek without fear of breaking anything. The museum consists of over 30 rescued historical buildings from the South of England, which have been faithfully and meticulously re-erected. The result is a delightful and informative taste of what the environment of rural and small-town England used to be like to live and work in. In many places it is vividly brought to life as you will find people dotted

> **"You are free to wander, explore and play hide and seek without fear of breaking anything"**

around the site demonstrating the various activities that would have been going on; wood-turning here, spinning or broom-making there.

Many of the buildings are clustered together in a grouping near the entrance. There is a treadwheel drawing water from a well in a wicker shed and a hands-on gallery with lots of touchy-feely boxes, weights and pulleys to be explored. Further on you will find several re-created artisan workshops – plumbing, joinery and wood-working, and a saw pit with huge saws, as well as shops, houses and other buildings from the 15th to 19th century. Highlights include the brick house, where you can play making patterns with traditional bricks, and the working water mill, where you can watch the wheat being ground between huge grit millstones into creamy-coloured stoneground flour. Kids have a chance here to taste the freshly-milled flour – you can buy the flour too, or biscuits made from it. The wheat is also sold as duck food for the many varieties of ducks and geese who live noisily on the adjacent millpond.

Follow the track away from the mini town for a lovely walk through the valley bottom and surrounding woodland. It can be done with a pushchair and takes in traditional cottages and barns, a village school and shepherds' huts. Our children loved exploring: the tiny beds and cots and the toilet and privy arrangements entralled them. They were awed at the idea of 4 or 5

children sharing one small iron bed. The medieval Bayleaf Farm is well worth a visit: it had an authentic wood fire in the centre of the hall and candle-making in progress when we visited. Nip upstairs for a demonstration of bed-making techniques of old! It also has traditional farm gardens and animals, including wallowing pigs and Shire horses. Further on you can walk through woods and discover a charcoal-burners camp.

There is a refreshment area near the millpond. It is closed November to March. You can eat inside a nearby cottage, with open window slats letting in sparrows. There are also plenty of picnic tables and benches around, or you may eat your own food anywhere in the grounds, except inside the houses (it attracts mice).

As you can always duck into a nearby building, you can come here in unsettled weather. In October, there was a lovely smell of wood smoke drifting through the air and autumn leaves to kick through. It can get busy in the summer, but there is plenty of space to escape into.

Fact File

● ADDRESS: Weald & Downland Open Air Museum, Singleton, Chichester, Sussex
● TELEPHONE: 01243 811348
● WEBSITE: www.wealddown.co.uk
● DIRECTIONS: A3 then A286 to Midhurst and Chichester. Signposted from Singleton village (midway between Midhurst and Chichester)
● PUBLIC TRANSPORT: Train to Chichester from Waterloo, then number 260 bus to Singleton, which runs about every 40 minutes
● DISTANCE: 50 miles
● TRAVEL TIME: 1 hour 30 minutes
● OPENING: Daily from February half term to end of October, 10.30am-6.00pm. Weekends and Wednesdays from 1st November to mid February, 10.30am-4.00pm
● PRICES: £6.00 adults, £3.00 children, under-5's free, family £15.00
● RESTAURANT FACILITIES: Yes
● NAPPY CHANGING FACILITIES: Yes
● HIGH CHAIRS: No
● DOGS: Yes
● PUSHCHAIR-FRIENDLY: Yes
● NEARBY: The Horse and Groom pub in Singleton has a family room and play area. Midhurst is a pretty, small town with tea shops. Goodwood Racecourse is within a few miles (01243 774107)

Up, Down, There & Back

The Bluebell Railway

And she blew, Whoo-oo-oo!

THERE WILL BE ENOUGH BELLS RINGING, STEAM HISSING AND SMOKE blowing down on the Bluebell Line to satisfy even the most ardent Thomas the Tank Engine enthusiast. For older train-spotters, a trip on the Bluebell Railway really conjures up the mythical Golden Age of steam. Be warned, it can be very busy at peak weekends (avoid Mother's Day). However, it does run all year and is a good trip to do in the winter, or a good option in wet weather.

> **"Walk right alongside the locomotive, watching the fires being stoked and the pistons throbbing"**

It consists of a reclaimed stretch of railway line running between East Grinstead and Sheffield Park Station (near Haywards Heath). Volunteers have lovingly amassed a wonderful collection of old steam trains and station memorabilia, and you can take rides up and down the line in old carriages pulled by restored steam trains. You can join the train at Kingscote, Horsted Keynes or Sheffield Park stations. The best place to start is probably Kingscote, but as there is no car access there you must catch the 473 bus from East Grinstead train station – a 10-minute ride(return fare £1.50 adult, 75p child).

Kingscote is a pretty little station in 1940's style. A glowing coal fire in the Booking Office adds to the nostalgia created by the cokey smell of steam trains all around, whilst the platform is a bustling flurry of people and announcements as the trains arrive and depart. Be prepared to mingle with an incongruous mix of delighted children and anoraked train-spotters.

We got straight on a train and were treated to a dose of instant nostalgia: remember that smoky smell of brown velveteen seats, sliding windows you can just manage to peep out of, and mirrors in the carriages where you could check your first attempts at make-up? Meanwhile, children will love the thrill of doors slamming, whistles blowing and the guard waving his green flag, before the train chugs slowly through beautiful Sussex countryside.

The trip to Horsted Keynes station takes about 15 minutes. This station is an authentic re-creation of the bygone heyday of the railways, complete with a coffin carrier and mounds of leather-bound suitcases and trunks. You can get off for a look round, good views of the comings and goings of trains, or for walks in the woods (good for bluebells in May). The footpath starts up near the top of the car park and is muddy after wet weather.

Back on the train and on to Sheffield Park station. This is the busiest station on the line and there is plenty to amuse young children. Stroll over the iron footbridge and look down on the engines busying backwards and forwards, or stopping to be refilled with water from an enormous water pipe. On the opposite platform, there is a small museum of train and station memorabilia and a model railway of Horsted Keynes in the 1920's. Take a peep into the gleaming signals box with labelled handles, and walk right alongside the locomotive, watching the fires being stoked and the pistons throbbing. At the rear of the station is the locomotive shed, where you can walk between the rails right next to the collection of amazingly huge engines and carriages.

Eating facilities are good. At Sheffield Park station you have the choice of a reproduction Victorian pub or a self-service cafe upstairs. At Horsted Keynes, there is an original 1882 station buffet. Some trains have cream teas and ploughman's lunches, but if you really feel like lashing out, book onto one of the Pullman carriages on Sunday trains offering lunches or cream teas (01825 722008). Alternatively, there are picnic spots at all the stations and picnic tables next to the platforms.

Trains run at intervals of between 45 and 90 minutes, depending on the time of year and day. A round trip takes about an hour and a half. Special events held during the year include a steam gala, a vintage transport fair and Xmas specials at Christmas (must be booked).

Fact File

● ADDRESS: The Bluebell Railway, Sheffield Park Station, near Uckfield, East Sussex
● TELEPHONE: 01825 723777 (bookings and enquiries) 01825 722370 (24 hour information)
● WEBSITE: www.bluebell-railway.co.uk
● DIRECTIONS: M23 and A23, leave at the junction with the A272 at Bolney. Follow the brown Bluebell Railway signs from there
● PUBLIC TRANSPORT: Train to Haywards Heath, with bus connections to Sheffield Park (ring the number above for details). Train to East Grinstead from Victoria, and connecting vintage bus to Kingscote
● DISTANCE: 45 miles
● TRAVEL TIME: 1 hour 30 minutes
● OPENING: Trains run at weekends throughout the year. Daily from 17 April to the end of September, and over Easter, school holidays and December (must be pre-booked). Sheffield Park station open daily all year
● PRICES: Admission and unlimited travel on day, adults £7.80, children £3.90, under-3's free, family £21.00
● RESTAURANT FACILITIES: Yes
● NAPPY CHANGING FACILITIES: Yes
● HIGH CHAIRS: Yes
● DOGS: Yes
● PUSHCHAIR-FRIENDLY: Yes
● NEARBY: Sheffield Park Gardens, about a mile from Sheffield Park, are beautiful National Trust gardens (01825 790231). Not open in the winter

Colne Valley Railway

IF A TASTE OF LUXURY APPEALS TO YOU, VISIT THIS RECONSTRUCTED railway. As you approach it, though, the view of clapped-out trains and decrepit railway equipment may lead you to think that you have arrived at the wrong place: a short walk from the parking area to the lovingly restored station puts to rest any such doubts. Here you will find all the steam trains, Pullmans and carriages to keep even the youngest train enthusiast entertained for several hours.

Located in a delightful, secluded spot in the Essex countryside, the Colne Valley Railway is the vision of two railway fans who wanted to re-create the atmosphere of a typical Essex country branch line of yesteryear. Built and staffed entirely by volunteers, it consists of Castle Hedingham station, a working signal box and a mile of track which once formed part of the Colne Valley and Halstead Railway. Every effort has been made to make the railway authentic, with the buildings, bridges and working signalbox modelled or re-constructed from local stations and railways.

> "Sit right up behind the driver and get a driver's-eye view of the track as you trundle along"

There is a large stock of working steam trains, diesels and a multitude of passenger carriages and wagons. During the open season, trains run on steam days between 12noon and 4.00pm for a 20-minute round trip. On a non-steam day you may be able to get a ride on a diesel: children love this as they can sit right up behind the driver and get a driver's-eye view of the track as you trundle along. With only one mile of track, the train ride itself is a bit short, although you can do as many return trips as you like and it is a very pretty trip, running through woodland and along the banks of the River Colne, with all the usual steam, flags and whistles. The engine drivers are there to talk to and you can see the signal box in operation.

On non-steam days the entrance fee is reduced and all the carriages, engines and buildings are open for viewing. Children can explore the engines (if you don't mind how dirty they get!), and you can walk along the track.

Pride and joy of the fleet must be the Pullman train, though. It consists of three historic carriages in luxurious Orient Express style, including a first-class restaurant offering Sunday lunches (book in advance). It may be difficult to justify all afternoon at the dining table to your children, who will probably be more keen to explore than eat. We took the less luxurious, but more child-friendly option, of the buffet car facilities at the station, where you can get light snacks and drinks in a more convenient atmosphere, albeit with a less sumptuous menu. There is also a picnic area in the adjoining woodland, with tables in the summer, from where you can watch the trains roll by. Be prepared to lug your pushchair up the steps of the passenger bridge to cross the tracks. Maybe you won't need the buggy anyway – best to let little legs tire themselves out running up and down the platform and have a peaceful journey home yourself, whilst your youngsters dream of being railway engineers.

For a change from the trains you can now visit the new Colne Valley Farm Park alongside the railway. This is set in peaceful water meadows and has a good collection of farm animal favourites: pigs, sheep, goats and cattle. You can wander through the pens meeting the animals, but it is a bit rough underfoot for pushchairs. Go on along the banks of the river for a pleasant ramble before returning to the railway for a cream tea and more train rides!

Fact File

- ADDRESS: Colne Valley Railway, Castle Hedingham, Halstead, Essex
- TELEPHONE: 01787 461174
- WEBSITE: www.cvr.org.uk
- DIRECTIONS: Exit 8 from the M11, then the A120 to Braintree, and follow the A131 towards Halstead. Signposted from Halstead, five miles north west on the A604 Cambridge to Colchester road
- PUBLIC TRANSPORT: None
- DISTANCE: 60 miles
- TRAVEL TIME: 1 hour 30 minutes
- OPENING: Static days all year. Steam days every Sunday from 26 March to 22 October, and mid week at Easter, half terms and during the summer
- PRICES: Steam days £6.00 adults, £3.00 children, under-3's free, family £15.00. Half price on non-steam days
- RESTAURANT FACILITIES: Yes
- NAPPY CHANGING FACILITIES: No
- HIGH CHAIRS: No
- DOGS: No
- PUSHCHAIR-FRIENDLY: No
- NEARBY: Castle Hedingham castle (01787 460261)

Hollycombe Steam Collection & Gardens

Mind You Hold On Tight!

HOLLYCOMBE IS A BRILLIANT DAY OUT. DESPITE IT POURING THE FIRST time we went, we had a marvellous time and have returned since to be equally impressed. It's an old-fashioned fairground, with all the noise, fun and excitement you'd expect, plus steam train rides, gardens to walk in and plenty of great picnicing spots. Don't miss it: there's heaps to do and to choose from.

First there is the fairground, with all the traditional rides: a galloping horses roundabout, big wheel, razzle dazzle tilt wheel, steam yachts and swing boats. Furnaces roar, smoke billows and pistons tremble, all practically drowned out when the fairground organ bursts into life with a tremendous "Tra-la-la-bom-bom, Bom-bom, Boom-babaa!".

"An old-fashioned fairground, with all the noise, fun and excitement you'd expect"

The entry ticket allows unlimited rides so you can keep coming back until your stomach can stand it no longer. The big wheel in particular is a real thrill –"Aaargh!" – remind yourself how scared you used to be as a child when you went on it!

Kids can go on some rides; the helter-skelters, ghost house and chain-swings were popular with our mob, and for young children there are several juvenile rides (strict notices inform that adults are not permitted on these!). Toddlers will be spoilt for choice on the roundabout; is it to be the fire engine with ladder and bell, the double decker bus or the aeroplane this time?

As it is all run by volunteers, you will find lots of

overall-clad enthusiasts with coal-smeared hands and smutty faces busy around the gleaming engines, getting into the spirit of things, or extolling the virtues of steam power. So if you want to find out more about any particular ride, just ask . . .

When you want a change from the fairground, there are three different train rides to pick from. The longest is a mile and a half ride on a narrow gauge railway, pulled by Jerry the locomotive. This passes through woodland, along a ridge with wonderful views of the South Downs, and even through a tunnel. Then there is a miniature railway, with its own station and clock tower, and finally,

the huge Commander B locomotive (lots of puff and whistles) which pulls two carriages along a short standard gauge railway. All have protection from the rain in covered carriages, should you need it.

There is also a steam tractor and trailer which takes you down to the farm, where you can see a plough and working steam farm equipment, as well as some farm animals. Finally, there are the gardens: mostly woodland, with great views, and wonderful azaleas and daffodils in the Spring, where you can go for a lovely walk whilst your children explore.

Although the steam equipment doesn't get going until 2.00pm, you can go in earlier to walk in the gardens or have something to eat in the cafe. This offers basic refreshments such as drinks, sandwiches and pasties. The gift shop sells souvenirs, toys, postcards and general train items.

Fact File

- ADDRESS: Hollycombe Steam Collection, Iron Hill, Liphook, Hampshire
- TELEPHONE: 01428 724900 and 01420 474740
- DIRECTIONS: A3 to Liphook. Signposted and about 2 miles drive from A3
- PUBLIC TRANSPORT: Train from Waterloo or Clapham Junction to Liphook. Hollycombe is about 1 mile from Liphook Station, an uphill walk along a lane with no footpath or get a taxi from the station
- DISTANCE: 45 miles
- TRAVEL TIME: 1 hour
- OPENING: Sundays and Bank Holidays from 2 April to 22 October. Daily from 23 July to 28 August. From about 1.00pm-6.00pm
- PRICES: Adults £6.50, children £5.00, under-2's free, saver £20.00
- RESTAURANT FACILITIES: Yes
- NAPPY CHANGING FACILITIES: No
- HIGH CHAIRS: No
- DOGS: No
- PUSHCHAIR-FRIENDLY: Yes
- NEARBY: The Devil's Punchbowl at Haslemere is great for walks and picnics

Kent & East Sussex Steam Railway

THIS MUST BE ONE OF THE PRETTIEST OF THE STEAM RAILWAYS, WITH immaculate liveried carriages, picturesque turn-of-the-century rural stations and classic English countryside scenery. If, like our children, yours just love going on the train, then you will not fail to be charmed by a visit here.

The trains run between Tenterden in Kent and Bodiam in East Sussex, via Northiam. It is a ten-mile stretch, lovingly-restored by volunteers, with a collection of three or four steam trains and carriages. Although we started from Tenterden you could just as well go from Northiam if you wanted: both have plenty of parking. New in 2000 is the availability of combined tickets with Bodiam Castle (see page 102).

Tenterden station itself is very attractive, but no doubt your children will be more interested in the train puffing and sighing

> ## "Passing reed beds and lily ponds, you ride above the level of the land"

on the platform. If you time it right (trains generally leave on the hour, but check in advance) you can do what we did and leap straight on. Pride of the fleet is a Victorian train of coaches, which you can see at Tenterden station if you don't manage to ride on them. We got into the 1950's red and cream carriages (apparently nicknamed 'blood and custard' by passengers at the time), which offer First Class coaches for 50p extra per person and give you the chance to have a bit of extra padding and wood-panelled interior. Very grand – but we opted for third class as we'd decided to picnic on the train and didn't want to be embarrassed by our 11-month-old smearing egg sandwiches on the upholstery!

The train pulls you out of Tenterden through Kent farmland resplendent with hops and oast houses. After the first stop at Rolvenden, the countryside opens out into a glorious coastal hinterland of small rivers, canals and waterways. Passing reed beds and lily ponds, you ride above the level of the land and get a wonderful view. We spotted herons, waving fishermen and enormous dragonflies. Also just one rabbit, which considering the extent of rabbit warrens alongside the track was somewhat surprising. (Your children may enjoy knowing that this stretch of the line was the inspiration for a Thomas the Tank Engine story.)

After 50 minutes' ride, the train puffs into Bodiam.

There is a 15-minute turnaround here, so you can get out and inspect the engine and chat to the driver, before getting back on, or you can stay and wait for the next train about an hour later. Facilities include toilets and a small buffet. The castle is a 5-minute walk from the station, and you can picnic up near there. You can also get off at Wittersham Road and Northiam where there are picnic areas, or Rolvenden, where you can watch the maintenance work from a viewing platform.

On the way back to Tenterden you can muse on the isolation of the stations, which really are planted in the middle of nowhere. In fact this partly explains the post-war demise of the line, because having been deliberately built away from all the villages in the 1900's, later it suffered from lack of traffic. As you rattle along, the children doing gymnastics on the seats, it makes you wonder which of our modern train routes will be mere tourist attractions in 50 years' time.

Back at Tenterden, there is plenty of bustle and commerce. You'll find a gift shop (for those essential Thomas the Tank bits), an adventure playground, small museum, restaurant and a video exhibition showing the history of the line. With the level crossing and signal box to admire, and trains coming and going all day, you could easily keep everyone amused for an hour or two. Special events run throughout the season.

To blow away any cobwebs after the railway, drive on down to the coast, where at Winchelsea beach, kids can run around to their hearts content, playing with stones and shells, whilst you ponder on the view of Dungeness power station on the horizon. To really treat yourselves, stop off at Rye though. The steep, narrow, cobbled streets, clap-boarded houses and small boat marina are appealing to all. There are lots of antique and craft shops, which you may not get a chance to visit with children, and plenty of tea shops and fish and chips restaurants (which you will!). It would probably be best at the end of the day, when it is quieter and you'll have more room on the narrow pavements. It makes a long day, but well worth the effort.

Fact File

- ADDRESS: Kent & East Sussex Railway, Tenterden Town Station, Tenterden, Kent
- TELEPHONE: 01580 762943 (talking timetable) or 01580 765155
- WEBSITE: www.seetb.org.uk/kesr
- DIRECTIONS: M20 (junction 9) exit for Ashford, and then the A28 to Tenterden. Signposted from the centre of the village
- PUBLIC TRANSPORT: Train to Ashford or Hastings, then bus to Tenterden. Bus information on 01634 281100 or 0870 243 3711
- DISTANCE: 70 miles
- TRAVEL TIME: 2 hours
- OPENING: Daily April to October. Sundays in remaining school holidays and other months. Train times vary, generally 10.30am-4.30pm
- PRICES: Adult £6.80, children £3.40, under-3's free, family £18.50. Unlimited travel (except on Bank Holidays and special event days)
- RESTAURANT FACILITIES: Yes
- NAPPY CHANGING FACILITIES: Yes
- HIGH CHAIRS: No
- DOGS: Yes
- PUSHCHAIR-FRIENDLY: Yes
- NEARBY: Rare Breeds Centre at Woodchurch (01233 861493). Steam river boat trips run from Northiam to Bodiam (01797 280363)

Leighton Buzzard Railway

THIS SMALL-SCALE, CHILD-SIZED, LITTLE RAILWAY DIFFERS FROM OTHER steam train rides in that most of the locomotives and carriage stock are rescued from industrial usage. Indeed, one of the best times to come is on one of the Industry Days (generally the second Sunday in the month), because then you can see specialised rolling stock carrying out the operations that it was designed for: peat wagons, sand transportation, munitions work and forestry operations. It's all pretty grimy stuff – just what kids like. If your children get excited about road works, then they will love seeing the huge 10RB diggers (giant mechanical excavators) doing their stuff here.

Originally a narrow gauge sand quarry railway, the line has been rescued and restored since its closure in the 1970's. Nowadays there are 10 steam engines in total owned by the line, six of which are working. On operational days you can do an hour's return trip on the railway, but there are plenty of other things to keep you amused, so don't be snobbish; grab your sarnies and make a day of it!

"Always lots of little locos shunting backwards and forwards"

Start off at the tiny Page's Park station, which is located in a park on the outskirts of Leighton Buzzard. The station consists of a ticket office, small shop and buffet. What it lacks in facilities is made up for by the friendly and enthusiastic staff – if you do the Santa Special in December you will find a welcoming coal fire.

With two tree-lined platforms overlooking the narrow line, and a grassy bank to sit on, we happily watched the comings and goings of Elf, Alice and P C Allen as they chugged in and out with the usual sighs, puffs and whistles you get on steam rides. The ride itself is in

covered carriages, and goes rather unglamorously through
back gardens to start with which amused us, but of
course the children didn't notice! You cross two level
crossings, complete with a man with a red flag and
astonished car drivers, before you get out into more open
countryside, with fields, cows and hedgerows to admire.

The terminus at Stonehenge Works is about two and a
half miles down the line. You get off here whilst the
engine does a 10-minute turnaround, however, it is worth
stopping longer and getting the next train back, although
do check in advance that there will be seating capacity
on the return trip. Here at Stonehenge is the real grunge
and grime associated with industrial railways. The

workshop has expanded around a former stable building and now is an engineering base for the railway line – a workshop in the true sense of the word. There are always lots of little locos shunting backwards and forwards, a plethora of engine bits and pieces, engine cabins to scramble in and over, a visitor centre, and on the Industry Days, all sorts of equipment in working mode. As at Page's Park station, there are plenty of knowledgeable and patient volunteers.

Back at Page's Park, the park next to the station offers plenty of potential for a picnic and running around, and there is an excellent children's play area. Walk the half mile down to the Grand Union canal and watch the boats coming and going, or even take a trip yourself: the Leighton Lady (01525 384563) offers short trips on the canal and will give you a chance to see locks in operation too.

Fact File

● ADDRESS: Leighton Buzzard Railway, Page's Park Station, Billington Road, Leighton Buzzard, Bedfordshire
● TELEPHONE: 01525 373888
● WEBSITE: www.btinternet.com/buzzrail
● DIRECTIONS: Exit 11 on the M1, through Dunstable, taking the A5 towards Milton Keynes, and turn off into Leighton Buzzard. Follow the brown Narrow Gauge Railway signs from Leighton Buzzard
● PUBLIC TRANSPORT: 45 minutes' walk from Leighton Buzzard train station (trains from Euston)
● DISTANCE: 40 miles
● TRAVEL TIME: 1 hour
● OPENING: Sundays, Easter and Bank Holiday weekends from 19 March to 29 October 11.15am-3.45pm. Some weekdays in June, July and August
● PRICES: Return trip adults £5.00, children £1.50, under-2's free
● RESTAURANT FACILITIES: No
● NAPPY CHANGING FACILITIES: No
● HIGH CHAIRS: No
● DOGS: Yes
● PUSHCHAIR-FRIENDLY: Yes
● NEARBY: Mead Open Farm (01525 852954)

The Watercress Line

THE STATION MASTER 'TOOT-TOOTS' HIS WHISTLE, THE GUARD SMARTLY waves a green flag, and with a gasp of steam and a belching cloud of billowing white smoke, the huge locomotive heaves us out of the station. We're off!

If your children like the noise, bustle and excitement of real steam trains, then the Watercress Line is a must. It is a restored 10-mile stretch of railway running between Alton and Alresford in a beautiful rural part of Hampshire. There are currently three locomotives working, two steam and one diesel, as well as seven others in various stages of restoration. The four stations on the line, Alton, Medstead and Four Marks, Ropley and Alresford, are all preserved and authentically recreate different periods in the railway's history, from the Twenties, to the late Fifties. Station staff wear appropriate uniforms, whilst decoration and equipment are in keeping with the period. Our kids loved it, especially being able to go inside the engine cab and see all the shining knobs and dials.

> **"Go inside the engine cab, and see all the shining knobs and dials"**

For a good day out, start at Alton mainline station and catch the steam train to Alresford: rather incongruously the platforms adjoin the commuter station. The journey takes about half an hour, with the train travelling through some lovely countryside as well as deep wooded cuttings. Alresford, when you get there, is a charming small town, with a lovely Georgian High Street, and several shops including antique and second-hand books (some open on Sundays). Have lunch outside at the Swan Hotel on the corner, or take a secret walk back to the station via the churchyard to catch a train back to Ropley, where you can picnic above the railway line and watch the trains go by (marquee provided for wet weather). It is worth spending some time at Ropley in the afternoon to see the engine shed with locomotives in the process of being restored – lots of grimy excitement. There is also a children's play area there. You can stop at the other stations too: from Four Marks station there are two signposted woodland walks which are about a mile long. Great picnic potential here, but limited access with pushchairs.

If you fancy a cream tea, take the Countryman special back to Alton (you need to book this in advance). If you have time, you can have an enjoyable walk round Alton (pick up a walk description leaflet at the station) including feeding the ducks on Kings Pond, a five-minute walk from the station.

The Line is run by volunteers and everyone we encountered was very enthusiastic and helpful. There are buffet facilities on most trains and at the station restaurant in Alresford, as well as snacks at the station shops at Alton and Ropley. The shops sell the usual souvenirs and postcards. Nappy changing facilities are available at Alresford, elsewhere there are the usual station toilet facilities. The steps over the railway line at Alton were a bit awkward with a pushchair, and the trains themselves are bit narrow (single pushchairs okay, but double buggies beware).

Fact File

● ADDRESS: The Watercress Line, Alresford Station, Hampshire
● TELEPHONE: 01962 733810/734200. Timetable 01962 734866
WEBSITE: www.watercressline.co.uk
● DIRECTIONS: A3 and A31 to Alton. Parking facilities at Alton and Alresford (pay and display)
● PUBLIC TRANSPORT: Regular train service from Waterloo to Alton
● DISTANCE: 45 miles
● TRAVEL TIME: 1 hour 30 minutes
● OPENING: Sundays in February, weekends from April to October. Weekdays at Easter, half terms and during the summer
● PRICES: Adults £8.00, children £5.00, under-5's free, family £26.00
● RESTAURANT FACILITIES: Yes
● NAPPY CHANGING FACILITIES: Yes
● HIGH CHAIRS: No
● DOGS: Yes
● PUSHCHAIR-FRIENDLY: Yes
● NEARBY: Alton and Alresford are both pleasant towns to walk around. The Devil's Punchbowl at Haselmere (20 miles away) is a great picnic and walks area

The Sun Has Got His Hat On

Ham House

*Go, said the bird, for the leaves
were full of children
Hidden excitedly, containing
laughter.*

FOR ONE OF THE BEST-KEPT SECRETS IN LONDON VISIT HAM HOUSE
on a hot summer's weekend to picnic, stroll by the river
and peacefully while away the afternoon. Within such
easy striking distance of the Capital, it remains
delightfully tranquil, but with the bustle and activity of the
river bank and Ham Polo Club nearby to offer some
amusement once you tire of your picnic.

Park next to the river and muster the troops and
equipment for the five-minute walk along the riverbank
footpath into the House, or back along the main driveway.
Head around the side of the House, by the old stable
block (now a National Trust shop), and into the Rose
Garden. This is the only place you can picnic within Ham
House grounds, but who needs more? It is a large,
grassy, enclosed garden, with a huge spreading oak in the
middle offering shade, and a myriad of roses rambling
heartily over the old stone walls. There is plenty of room
to spread your blanket, unpack the hamper, and
peacefully soak up the summer. No dogs, ball games or
radios are allowed.

If you stray outside the walls of the Garden, you'll find
yourselves in the main gardens of the House. With formal
hedges, sundials, statuary, gravel paths and low walls,
they are well worth a visit. There is also a wilderness

garden with high hedges and trees for playing hide and seek.

The House itself is open 1.00pm-5.00pm Saturdays to Wednesdays from the beginning of April to the end of October. It is a graceful 17th century house with fine furniture, pictures and textiles within. Pushchairs, backpacks and high heels are not permitted inside.

All the facilities you need can be found in the grounds with toilets, gift shop and restaurant next to the Rose Garden. The restaurant has a garden room and tables

"A huge spreading oak offering shade, and a myriad of roses rambling heartily over the old stone walls"

☞

outside where you can take tea and watch the squirrels. The restaurant has the same opening periods as the main house.

When your children become curious about the muted sounds of loudspeaker announcements in the distance, stroll back to the main entrance of the house, follow your ears on the path parallel to the river and onto Ham Common. On most summer Sundays you'll find Ham Polo Club in action from about 2.30pm. Sleek, sweating horses, immaculate riders, spirited manoeuvring and stamping will keep everyone amused for a while.

Return along the river footpath where it is much busier and you can watch the boats plying up and down the river and the World and His Wife out to play. If you fancy it, you can even take Hammerton's foot ferry across to the Twickenham side of the river, where there is a small children's playground and the grounds of Marble Hill House. The ferry ride takes four minutes, and there is a small charge. It runs daily from 10.00am to 6.00pm or 6.30pm at weekends: if it doesn't appear shout loudly to attract the ferryman's attention!

Fact File

● ADDRESS: Ham House, Ham, Richmond, Surrey
● TELEPHONE: 0208 940 1950
● WEBSITE: www.nationaltrust.org.uk
● DIRECTIONS: North/South circular to Richmond, follow the A307 to Petersham and signs to Ham House
● PUBLIC TRANSPORT: Bus (0207 222 1234) or train (0207 928 5100) to Richmond (30-minute walk) or Kingston (40-minute walk). River bus from Richmond Sundays, May to September (0208 546 2434)
● DISTANCE: 15 miles
● TRAVEL TIME: 45 minutes
● OPENING: Garden Saturday to Wednesday, 10.30am-6.00pm or dusk
● PRICES: Garden £1.50 adults, 75p children, £3.00 family. House and garden £5.00 adults, £2.50 children, £12.50 family. Free to National Trust members
● RESTAURANT FACILITIES: Yes
● NAPPY CHANGING FACILITIES: Yes
● HIGH CHAIRS: CHECK
● DOGS: No
● PUSHCHAIR-FRIENDLY: Yes
● NEARBY: National Trust's Osterley Park for park, pleasure gardens and elegant Adam's mansion (0208 560 3918)

Kew Gardens

IF YOU THINK THAT THE ROYAL BOTANIC GARDENS AT KEW ARE JUST
for ardent plant spotters discussing the merits of different
chrysanthemum species, think again, because they are
ideal for a day's picnic, and very easy to get to, both by
car and by public transport. One of Kew's strongest points
for those with young children is that it is dog-free, which
must make it one of the largest poo-free areas that you
can find. Despite being very popular at weekends, you
can still find far-flung corners that are to all intents and
purposes deserted, and in the week – well, you will
almost find the whole gardens at your disposal.

A mixture of wide, grassed areas and woodland areas,
the gardens are very extensive – you'd be hard-pushed to
cover everywhere in one day. Although there are some
formal flower displays, most of the gardens are pretty wild
in character, but do have lovely and wide pushchair-
friendly footpaths. There are
no nasty 'Keep off the grass'
notices, and you can romp
at will through shady dells
and woody glens. Dotted
around are information
boards to help you beef up
on your general knowledge
skills (do you know how
many oak trees it took to
build a sailing galleon, for
example?) and giving older

> ## "No nasty 'Keep off the grass' notices, and you can romp at will through shady dells and woody glens"

children a lot of fun and interest. Over at the quieter, far
side of the gardens, the paths border onto the banks of
the Thames, with the requisite fisherman gently passing
the day, and the occasional rowing eight.

The leaflet you are given at the entrance marks three
suggested walks. Our favourite is the West Walk, which is
the quietest and which has several little shelters and
alcoves for playing in. The other walks are the East Walk,
which includes the glasshouses and temples, and the
North Walk which takes in the 17th century gardens in

Kew Palace and those famous lilacs. There is something to see at any time of the year – bulbs, cherry blossom and lilacs in the spring; roses, giant water lilies and bedding plants in the summer; berries and autumn leaves to kick through in October and November; and Holly trees, Strawberry trees and camellias in the winter.

Should you tire of wandering in the gardens, there are always the glasshouses to pop into. The largest and most impressive are the Temperate House, where you can spot tangerines, grapefruits and avocados growing, and the steamy Palm House, with coconuts, date palms, bananas and giant bamboo. Both have walkways running high above the floor level so you can look down on the dizzy depths of tangled foliage before descending once again into the undergrowth of exotic scents and heady blooms. You'll have to leave pushchairs down at ground level though. In the basement of the Palm House there is a marine display of algae and fishes. You have to lift up young children to see inside many of the displays here.

Catering facilities are good in the summer, with a choice of cafes and kiosks selling the usual range of food and drinks. During the winter, there is less choice: during the week only the Orangery restaurant is open. On sunny Sundays you may have to queue up to a quarter of an hour for your food, and be prepared to share your table (and children's table manners!) with an unsuspecting member of the public. By far the best thing to do, though, is to bring a picnic, spread it out somewhere that takes your fancy, and enjoy the freedom of eating in the fresh air.

A couple of final points, as well as the ban on dogs, you are also not allowed to bring bikes, trikes or radios into the gardens, or play ball games. This may be a blessing to some, but a disappointment to others. If you come in the car there is a car park along by the river entrance.

Fact File

● ADDRESS: Royal Botanic Gardens, Kew, Richmond, Surrey
● TELEPHONE: 0208 940 1171 (answerphone), 0208 332 5622
● DIRECTIONS: Take the A205, South Circular to Kew, turning off and following the signs to Kew Gardens before you cross Kew Bridge
● PUBLIC TRANSPORT: Trains from Waterloo to Kew Bridge station and a 10-minute walk across Kew Bridge to the Gardens from the station. Alternatively the District line tube to Kew Gardens and then about a 5-minute walk. During summer, river boats run from Westminster (0207 930 2062)
● DISTANCE: 10 miles
● TRAVEL TIME: 30-45 minutes
● OPENING: Daily 9.30am-dusk. Glasshouses close about an hour earlier than gardens
● PRICES: £5.00 adults, £2.50 children, under-5's free. Family ticket £13.00
● RESTAURANT FACILITIES: Yes
● NAPPY CHANGING FACILITIES: Yes
● HIGH CHAIRS: Yes
● DOGS: No
● PUSHCHAIR-FRIENDLY: Yes
● NEARBY: Kew Bridge Steam Museum (0208 568 4757)

Littlehampton Beach

Oh, I do like to be beside the seaside!

GATHER YOUR BUCKETS AND SPADES, YOUR RUBBER RINGS AND YOUR beach balls: Littlehampton is a classic seaside trip for children. A fine, sandy beach exposed at low tide is complimented by small stones and shells further up which are a treasure-trove for shell-seekers. And there is lots more – sea and river trips, crabbing potential, a train ride along the promenade and a small funfair all combine to make Littlehampton a great summer's day out.

Head straight for the seafront as you come into the town for two large car parks, one at each end of the beach. At the western end, near the mouth of the River Arun, you will find all the trappings of the Great British Seaside Resort: fish and chips, shops selling beach paraphernalia, seaside rock, canoe rides and the funfair. On a sunny, hot day you will need to be prepared to rub shoulders with everyone else on the beach, especially as the tide comes in, and enjoy sharing spades, buckets and biscuits. A small road

"Acres of golden sand and a warm, shallow sea which is very safe for children"

train runs along the front for a 10-minute ride to the eastern end. This is quieter and where you will find grassy lawns (great if you don't want another Great British tradition – sandy sandwiches), a small play area, putting green and a cafe. Toilets are at the west end.

At low tide you will be able to enjoy acres of golden sand and a warm, shallow sea which is very safe for children. As the tide comes in, children can enjoy jumping off the groynes into the deepening water, and you will notice a feverish intensity about the sand-castle building. Check tide tables in advance (in the newspaper) to plan your day.

Whatever you do, don't miss a trip to the west end of the beach because the river mouth there offers all sorts of attractions. At high tide you can hang a fishing line (available at the seafront shops) over the edge of the river wall, suitably baited (raw bacon was the favoured tip when we went) and if you are lucky, catch dozens of small crabs. This provides endless amusement for children of all ages, and maybe the crabs too as some of them looked liked they had been caught and thrown back more than once! There are fishing boats plying up and down the river, loads of other small river craft and plenty of rotting hulls with their bows showing like skeletons in the mud.

☞ The river mouth is also the place to board a boat for a river trip up to Arundel, or a shorter trip round the harbour or along the coast. If your success with crabs has given you the bug, try the sea trip and hang a few mackerel lines off the boat. The boat trips are run by Skylark Cruises (01903 717337) and are in uncovered boats.

To get away from the crowds, take the small ferry across the river (small charge) to the West Beach Conservation area and Nature Reserve. This is much more tranquil, with sand dunes along the beach and wooded grassland behind. Pick up a leaflet describing the area and its two-hour nature route from the ferryman. It is a perfect picnic spot, and there is a small refreshment kiosk too. You can also reach it over a footbridge from the town, or drive round behind the town itself and come to it along the A259. Nude bathing is discouraged (which suggests you may encounter it), but no one objected to our children skinny-dipping!

Fact File

- ADDRESS: Littlehampton, West Sussex
- TELEPHONE: 01903 713480 (Tourist Information Office)
- DIRECTIONS: A24 from the north, or A27/M27 along the coast
- PUBLIC TRANSPORT: Hourly trains from Victoria taking about one hour 40 minutes
- DISTANCE: 60 miles
- TRAVEL TIME: One hour 30 minutes to two hours
- OPENING: Boat trips, ferry to West Beach and Tourist information May to September only
- PRICES: Free
- RESTAURANT FACILITIES: Yes
- NAPPY CHANGING FACILITIES: Yes, west end of beach
- HIGH CHAIRS: Some restaurants
- DOGS: Yes
- PUSHCHAIR-FRIENDLY: yes
- NEARBY: Arundel Castle (01903 883136)

Polesden Lacey

IF YOU LIKE DREAMING, TRY WANDERING AROUND THE GARDENS AT Polesden Lacey, and muse on how life would have been here 90 years ago – elegant ladies with parasols, fine dresses, delicate dishes and children safely tucked away with governesses. Then come back to earth with a jolt as your delightful offspring hurtle towards a muddy puddle or go puce in the face as you try to cajole them to put their gloves on.

Polesden Lacey is a beautiful Regency house, formerly owned by the playwright and politician Sheridan, which overlooks a wonderful secluded valley in the midst of Surrey. The grounds, consisting of both formal and wild areas, are great for walking in and picnicing with children, with lots of different structures and varying layouts to keep everyone amused. There are gravel paths through walled rose arbours, knot gardens with iris and lavender separated by box hedges (great for hide and seek), and rolling lawns and terraces with stunning views of the North Downs. It's full of little nooks and crannies that children will delight to explore – our family's favourite is the half-timbered, thatched bridge with steps up, and the occasional car passing in the lane below. The bridge leads to an orchard of lime and cherry trees, ideal for picnics, and with a little house at the end where the children mucked around for ages on our last visit.

> **"Full of little nooks and crannies that children will delight to explore"**

There are four waymarked walks you can do, ranging from a 1-mile stroll, passable with a pushchair, to longer and more strenuous walks up to 3 miles long. They all go through the woodland, fields and terraces that make up the estate. The kids will find plenty of small trees to climb and bushes to make dens in along the way. The more intrepid should ask for details of longer, guided walks with the wardens.

For something different and more relaxing (possibly!) you could try hiring a croquet set, which are available for games between May and September. Alternatively, just check out the other facilities: a restaurant with outside tables situated in a pretty courtyard (not always open though), a National Trust gift shop (quite a few children's toys and books) and toilets with a nappy change table. There are plenty of good picnic spots to settle in, although picnicing is not allowed on the main lawns around the house. You may also visit the house, but pushchairs would have to be left outside.

For a good day out, you could have lunch in one of the many nearby Surrey pubs. The White Horse at Shere, although not specifically catering for families, allows children in a side bar. It does good meals and has a lovely mellow atmosphere, with wood panelling, old oak beams and log fires in the winter. Shere itself is charming with small streets, teashops, antique shops and ducks cavorting in the stream running through the village – the only drawback is the large number of people there at weekends! There are several public footpaths from the village too: try going up behind the wonderfully quaint village church, and following the paths across the fields.

Fact File

- ADDRESS: Polesden Lacey, Bookham, near Dorking, Surrey
- TELEPHONE: 01372 458203 or 452048
- DIRECTIONS: Located just off the A246 between Leatherhead and Guildford. Signposted from Great Bookham
- PUBLIC TRANSPORT: None
- DISTANCE: 30 miles
- TRAVEL TIME: 45 minutes
- OPENING: Grounds are open daily all year 11.00am-6.00pm or dusk. The house is open afternoons only, and is restricted to certain days
- PRICES: Grounds adults £3.00, children £1.50, under-5's free. House £3.00 adults, £1.50 children
- RESTAURANT FACILITIES: Yes
- NAPPY CHANGING FACILITIES: Yes
- HIGH CHAIRS: Yes
- DOGS: Yes
- PUSHCHAIR-FRIENDLY: Yes
- NEARBY: Shere village or walks on the North Downs, around Box Hill

Scotney Castle Gardens

What light through yonder window breaks?

FOR THE VERY ESSENCE OF COURTLY ROMANCE, HIDEAWAYS AND CUBBY holes, twisting paths and unexpected hollows, come to Scotney Castle. You'll find moated medieval castle ruins with Tudor additions and a Romeo and Juliet balcony to boot! Surrounded by dreamy gardens and rambling countryside to picnic in, it makes a stunning day out in the Kent hills. Make sure you bring drinks in hot weather, as refreshments on site are practically non-existent.

Start off in the walled garden outside, where you park your car. Alongside are gnarled old trees and pleasant grassy areas to spread your picnic. If it seems a bit crowded – and it can be busy in the height of summer – carry on a few yards to the Estate grounds, where you'll find plenty of space on the open grassy slopes.

When you are ready, amble down to the entrance at the side of the National Trust shop and into the gardens themselves. For the first 100 yards or so, the path slopes steeply through a green tunnel of overhanging trees, before suddenly opening out with the castle appearing like a mirage in front of your eyes.

"We may not have met the Big Bad Wolf but we did find blackberries, acorns, feathers and dragonflies a-plenty"

Which way to go? Anyway you like, as long as you're still going downhill you'll get to the castle. Idle by the flower beds, hide in the little gullies, or peer over the low walls of the moat bridges at ripples of lurking water monsters (probably just goldfish). You don't have to keep to the paths – why walk when you can roll down a grassy slope?

There are two wings left to the castle, one of ruined walls open to the sky, and the second just like the crooked house in the nursery rhyme. It has an 'Alice through the Looking Glass' feel with its tiny rooms and random souvenirs from the centuries: spears and arrows on the walls, old-fashioned jelly moulds in the kitchen and bits of a Doodle-Bug and 2nd World War bomb. Our children's favourite was the secret series of interlocking rooms which are part of the priest's hole and delightfully child-sized. They could climb in and peer up where adults couldn't and shiver in delicious fear at the thought of being holed up inside. The stairs and small rooms make it unsuitable for pushchairs, but it is small enough for carrying non-walkers.

Outside again we admired the balcony overlooking the courtyard. Underneath is a delightful little arch leading to the older ruined part of the castle – the walls now wisteria-clad. Within, the gardens open into a large grassy lawn encirled by the moat. It's a great spot to linger, a haven of crab apple trees, giant rhubarb and a wonderful old mulberry tree which can be climbed, its twisted trunk full of crevices that our two-year-old solemnly stuffed with fruit from the tree whilst his brother and sister delightedly ran through and round the trailing branches. Be warned, although the area is small, there are opportunities to lose sight of children if you are not careful.

You can follow the path all round the moat, looking out for the boat house and Scotney dragon as you go, and up past the ice house to the top of the gardens again. Don't miss the quarry though: vertical rock faces with trees growing straight out the rock, slimy fern-covered walls and mossy steps. We spent ages hiding and "hullo-ing" in here.

For a breather after the confines of the garden, do one of the estate walks, which are open (and free) all year. They are described in a £1 leaflet available from the National Trust shop, but you can easily do the walks without as they are well-waymarked and along readily identifiable paths. There are two circular walks on offer: a short 30-minute woodland stroll, or a longer three-mile walk taking in ancient woods, fields, and gentle ups and downs. Both start from the car park. The longer of the two was delightfully secluded (we met only one other family who were contentedly laden with filled boxes of blackberries) and manageable with a pushchair (a bit stony in places and with a couple of stiles to be negotiated). It is a great, varied and accessible walk: we may not have met the Big Bad Wolf but we did find blackberries, acorns, feathers and dragonflies a-plenty.

Fact File

- ADDRESS: Scotney Castle Gardens, Lamberhurst, Kent
- TELEPHONE: 01892 891081
- WEBSITE: www.nationaltrust.org.uk
- DIRECTIONS: A21 south from M25, 8 miles south of Tunbridge Wells and just beyond Lamberhurst. Signposted on the left
- PUBLIC TRANSPORT: No
- DISTANCE: 45 miles
- TRAVEL TIME: 1 hour 20 minutes
- OPENING: Gardens 1 April to 29 October, Wednesday to Sunday, 11.00am-6.00pm weekdays, 2.00pm-6.00pm weekends.Closed Good Friday. Estate open all year
- PRICES: Gardens & Castle £4.00 adults, £2.00 children, under-5's free, family £10.00. Free to National Trust members. Estate free
- RESTAURANT FACILITIES: No
- NAPPY CHANGING FACILITIES: No
- HIGH CHAIRS: No
- DOGS: No
- PUSHCHAIR-FRIENDLY: Yes
- NEARBY: Bewl Water, a watersports and picnic area

Whitstable

But four young Oysters hurried up
All eager for the treat. . .

FOR A SOMEWHAT DIFFERENT DAY AT THE SEASIDE TO THE USUAL
amusement arcades, kiss-me-quick hats and fish and
chip bars, come to Whitstable. Easily accessible by train,
this quiet and unassuming sea port on the Thames
estuary offers a beach, a working harbour, and a
Lilliputian-scale village full of antique shops. All within an
environment of wheeling seagulls, distant ships on the
horizon and the distinctive sea smell of rotting seaweed!

The main beach, Tankerton Slopes, is a 15-minute
walk from the railway station, or there is plenty of parking
space nearby. Although a pebble beach, there are lovely
safe grassy slopes sweeping gently down to the
promenade and a wide
shelving seashore. With
lots of space, groynes to
scramble on and an
inexhaustible supply of
pebbles to play with, kids
can be quite happy for
hours and maybe you
could even try a swim
yourself. There is a small
cafe and tearooms and
public loos nearby.

> **"Lots of space, groynes to scramble on, and an inexhaustible supply of pebbles to play with"**

Walking back towards the town and harbour from the
beach, along Beach Walk and Tower Parade you pass
Whitstable Castle, a nineteenth century folly with
attractive gardens, and the Tea Rooms, open Thursdays,
Fridays and Sundays, which have gardens overlooking the
harbour. The harbour itself is a working port with all the
associated bustle of boats, cranes and machinery. The
activity, sights and smells are a treat for young children –
ours were fascinated by the cockle-shelling conveyor belt,
but you'll need to be vigilant with respect to sheer drops

☞

☞

into the water, quarry lorries coming and going and working equipment.

At the east end of the harbour there is the Oyster and Fishery exhibition, with memorabilia and displays of Whitstable's famous oyster industry. Here you can see a marine life display, or get your fingers wet in the seashore 'touch pool', and buy fresh oysters packed to take home. At the back is the Beachcombers Gardens seashore area where you can relax and picnic whilst the children poke around on the shore.

The town centre has a timeless air about it and consists of quaint narrow streets, clap-boarded fishermen's houses and period shops. Some of the narrow pavements can be a bit difficult to negotiate with

pushchairs, but if you leave the High Street and branch down one of the many alleys, you will get to the Sea and Island Walls which are easier to walk along with children.

If you don't picnic on the beach, family-friendly facilities in the town are a bit hard to come by. We lunched in the Old Neptune pub on the seafront, a very traditional white-painted old pub with wooden chairs and floors. It is one of the historical features of the town itself, worth looking at even if you don't eat there. It has a small outside patio with tables and chairs.

Whitstable Oyster Festival is a week-long extravaganza, usually the last week in July, with a traditional, costumed, landing parade, a mud run, lots of games and family events and a bevy of boats in the harbour. Why not give it a go?

Fact File

● ADDRESS: Whitstable, near Canterbury, Kent
● TELEPHONE: 01227 275482 (Tourist Information Centre), 01227 280753 (Oyster Exhibition)
● DIRECTIONS: Exit the M2 at junction 7, then the A299
● PUBLIC TRANSPORT: Trains from Victoria station every hour
● DISTANCE: 55 miles
● TRAVEL TIME: 1 hour 30 minutes
● OPENING: Oyster and Fishery Exhibition 10.00am-4.00pm daily from Easter holidays to October
● PRICES: Oyster Exhibition £1.50 adults, £1.00 children, under-5's free
● RESTAURANT FACILITIES: Yes
● NAPPY CHANGING FACILITIES: No
● HIGH CHAIRS: No
● DOGS: Yes
● PUSHCHAIR-FRIENDLY: Yes
● NEARBY: Blean Bird Park (01227 471666), or Canterbury (cathedral, walks and museums)

Windsor Town & Great Park

WINDSOR IS PERFECT FOR A PICNIC AND A REALLY FULL DAY — wonderful for the long days of summer. There is an almost endless choice of nearby picnic spots – Runnymede by the river; the rural tranquillity of the Great Park, where you can often catch polo matches in the summer; or the fields and pastures around Datchet.

As the Thames meanders gently through lush meadows past Windsor, our favourite spot is very close to the centre of Windsor, but is actually over the river in Eton. Cross over Windsor River Bridge to Eton, it is generally quieter than Windsor town there, and walk upstream along the towpath through The Brocas meadow. The broad, open meadow is everything a perfect picnic spot should be: soft, luxuriant grass with buttercups, daisies, clover and dandelions, the river gently lapping the banks, and spectacular views of Windsor Castle and Eton College as a backdrop. Sit on the banks and watch everyone messing about in boats – some vigilance is required here if your children are anything like ours – or pick a patch further back in the meadow, where it is more peaceful and shadier. Or just continue walking along the towpath through woods and pastures. Watch out for bicycles on the towpath though, as the coaches for the Eton College oarsmen pound along the bank shouting encouragement (or abuse) to the crews! (It may be quieter in a few years' time when the new rowing course is built upstream at Dorney, but then there won't be so much entertainment.)

Alternatively, stay on the Windsor side of the river and walk upstream along the promenade, past fishermen and

> "The broad, open meadow is everything a perfect picnic spot should be"

river boats, towards the Alexandra Gardens. You will see plenty of enthusiastic swans, ducks and geese to feed (if you want to lose your fingers!). About half a mile upstream from the bridge you can picnic in the gardens. There is a small toddler funfair nearby with about five or six rides. On a really hot day, the Alexandra Gardens have the advantage over the Eton side by offering lots of large, shady trees.

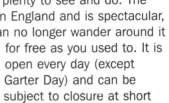

In Windsor town there is plenty to see and do. The Castle is the largest castle in England and is spectacular, although you can no longer wander around it for free as you used to. It is open every day (except Garter Day) and can be subject to closure at short notice (01753 831118 to check). The Changing of the Guard is at 11.00am daily from May to early August, and alternate days the rest of the year. If the weather is poor there are many museums – Queen Mary's Dolls House, the Royalty and Empire exhibition at the Windsor & Eton Central station, or perhaps the Household Cavalry Museum. If you fancy the sights, horse-drawn carriage rides go from the taxi stand outside Windsor castle, but are expensive.

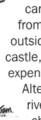

Alternatively, try a river boat (a bit cheaper), or an open top bus.

Periodically through the summer Windsor Great Park is the site for international and national polo matches. These could almost be a day out in themselves. All the glamour of a major sporting event, expensive cars, champagne, strawberries and picnic hampers, but without the crowds that are often so intimidating with young children. Even the busiest events are very accessible. Children are fascinated by the sprightly polo ponies, and there are usually horsey exhibitions and trade stands.

Park your car in one of the designated car parks (approximately £10.00 per car for an international event) and walk up with your picnic to large, free, grassy enclosures alongside the field. Alternatively, you can pay a lot more to go into one of the stands to rub shoulders with the cognoscenti. In summer, from around the start of May, polo is on every day except Monday, with matches two or three times a week, and major international events three times a year. All are held in the Guards Polo Club in the centre of the Park. Details are obtainable from the Polo Club (01784 434212).

Fact File

● ADDRESS: Windsor, Berkshire
● TELEPHONE: 01753 852010 (Tourist Information Centre)
● DIRECTIONS: M4 (junction 6) or M3 (junction 3) motorways. Parking in Windsor town can be difficult – try the station car parks, or along Meadow Lane on the Eton side of the river (in which case take junction 5, the Eton exit off the M4 and approach Eton through Datchet). For the Great Park, approach via Egham (junction 13 off the M25), and Old Windsor
● PUBLIC TRANSPORT: Trains from Waterloo to Windsor & Eton Riverside. Also trains from Paddington to Slough, and then a local train to Windsor & Eton Central Station
DISTANCE: 25 miles
● TRAVEL TIME: 1 hour
● OPENING: Anytime
● PRICES: Free (not castle)
● RESTAURANT FACILITIES: In the town
● NAPPY CHANGING FACILITIES: No
● HIGH CHAIRS: In the town
● DOGS: Yes
● PUSHCHAIR-FRIENDLY: Yes
● NEARBY: The Courage Shire Horse Centre(01628 824848)

Other Books IN THE SERIES

ALSO AVAILABLE IN THIS SERIES:

DAYS OUT WITH KIDS in the **Midlands**
TRIED-AND-TESTED FUN FAMILY
OUTINGS IN WARWICKSHIRE, WORCESTERSHIRE,
SHROPSHIRE, GLOUCESTERSHIRE, STAFFORDSHIRE,
LEICESTERSHIRE, AND WEST MIDLANDS.
132 PAGES, PAPERBACK, £4.99 ISBN 1-901411-249

DAYS OUT WITH KIDS in the **North West**
TRIED-AND-TESTED FUN FAMILY
OUTINGS IN LANCASHIRE, MERSEYSIDE,
DERBYSHIRE AND CHESHIRE.
132 PAGES, PAPERBACK, £4.99 ISBN 1-901411-222

DAYS OUT WITH KIDS in the **North East**
TRIED-AND-TESTED FUN FAMILY OUTINGS
IN NORTHUMBERLAND, DURHAM, CLEVELAND,
TYNE & WEAR AND NORTH YORKSHIRE.
140 PAGES, PAPERBACK, £4.99 ISBN 1-901411-265

DAYS OUT WITH KIDS in the **West Country**
TRIED-AND-TESTED FUN FAMILY OUTINGS IN
SOMERSET, DORSET, WILTSHIRE, AVON,
GLOUCESTERSHIRE, WORCESTERSHIRE,
HEREFORDSHIRE AND SOUTH WALES.
132 PAGES, PAPERBACK, £4.99 ISBN 1-901411-281

ALL OTHER BOOKS ARE AVAILABLE FROM BOOKSHOPS OR:

BON•BON VENTURES
24 ENDLESHAM ROAD
LONDON SW12 8JU
TEL: 0181 488 3011   FAX: 0181 265 1700

AND OUR WEB SITE **www.daysoutwithkids.co.uk**

PAYMENT MAY BE MADE BY CREDIT CARD (ACCESS/VISA/MASTERCARD), OR BY
CHEQUE /POSTAL ORDER PAYABLE TO BONBON VENTURES. PLEASE ALLOW
£1.00 POSTAGE AND PACKING FOR THE FIRST BOOK, AND 50P PER BOOK
FOR SUBSEQUENT BOOKS.

Website

Our DAYS OUT WITH KIDS website can be found on

www.daysoutwithkids.co.uk

It has lots of information on events at the attractions featured in this book, special offers and recommendations for trips all round the country. You can also use it to e-mail us with your comments on trips featured or your suggestions for new trips. We'd love to hear from you!

HAPPY DAYS OUT!